ENOUGH ROOM FOR JOY:

Jean Vanier's L'Arche:
A Message for Our Time.

ENOUGH ROOM FOR JOY:

Jean Vanier's L'Arche:
A Message for Our Time.

Bill Clarke, S.J.

McClelland and Stewart Limited

CONTENTS

DEDICATION

To my mother
in gratitude for all that she is
and for all that she has
given me out of her immense love
and profound peace.

Foreword

I have just finished reading Bill's book and my heart is filled with thanksgiving. Sometimes my memory fails before the pressures of the present. It is good to relive what God has done in His Arche. For it is true, this is His work and not ours.

There is yet much opaqueness in our communities, as in myself, as in each of us. Many things that prevent the Spirit living freely. But I know that Jesus came to heal and to pardon. Also, there have been many deep failures. I think with sadness of the seven men and women we put back into the psychiatric hospital in spite of promises made to them. God knows our weaknesses.

Bill has accentuated the joys and the sufferings and our fragility, but he has rarely spoken of our real weaknesses and infidelities. It is true that it is not easy for him to do so, not because these are not evident, but because of his reverence for others. We have yet a lot to learn, and even more, we must deepen daily our love and our professional skills.

Yes, I am thankful for the past, I rejoice in the present and I await the future with expectancy and confidence.

I trust that as we evolve . . . and God knows things are changing so fast at l'Arche and the Arches throughout the world – we will remain faithful to our call: live day by day in mutual love and acceptance, dependent upon the Spirit striving to form *one* community, open to new expansion and to welcoming the most wounded, growing in competency to help all to grow.

Will you pray for that. Pray that as we become known through this book and others that we will keep that initial simplicity and poverty and a desire to be present to wounded people, to help them evolve and to evolve with them.

Please, do not feel that you must come to l'Arche to visit us – do not think that we are something special. There is a real danger today of our being overcome by visitors – good-willed and eager to help or to imitate us. Rather, in the silence of your heart join us in communion with the Spirit of God who is Love, Compassion and Truth. Commit yourselves to the wounded ones near you today. Listen to them, seek to be with them, grow with them in mutual respect and love. Then all of us can join hands spiritually and seek each in his own way to make our world a place of peace, of universal love and brotherhood where God is the Father of all men, however handicapped or intelligent they may be.

As my life calls me to assume new responsibilities, and to travel from country to country, I am acutely aware that others are *living* what I am but *preaching*. To talk I know is important. It is good that the message be known. But it is more important to live and to live fully as my brothers and sisters of l'Arche are living . . . to live in obscurity without fame only in love and tender compassion.

I thank Jesus for them, for Raphael, for Guru and so many. I thank Him for this family of which I am a part – for they have given me life.

Jean Vanier
Asha Niketan
Calcutta, India
December, 1973

Entering the village of Trosly-Breuil.

Meeting in the village square.

Matador: in the main street of the village.

(*top*) The Val Fleuri, largest of the l'Arche homes.
(*bottom*) Setting of the village, by Compiègne forest.

CHAPTER ONE

Getting Into the Ark

This book is about a new type of community that is rapidly spreading in different parts of the world, and which in a quiet way is calling to liberation people caught in, or victims of a world of excessive individualism and competition.

L'Arche began in France in 1964 to give a permanent home to mentally handicapped adults. It seeks to unite the handicapped and those who assist them in a single community, inspired by a spirit of loving acceptance that will help all its members develop to their fullest potential as human beings.

The word "l'Arche" is French for "the Ark." In the Bible story the Ark was where Noah gathered the whole motley range of God's creatures to save them from the flood. So the Ark is symbolic of a place of refuge, of a community of great variety, and of the gift of hope.

My first contact with this community was through its founder and director, Jean Vanier. This was in Montreal in the winter of 1964, at a national conference for university students engaged in the study of theology. The essence of Vanier's conferences was that the Church and society not only have a mission to minister to the poor but they very much need the poor. He spoke of how a certain group of "poor," the mentally handicapped, have much to give to others in a variety of ways. If the Church and society do not embrace these and other rejected people, neither of them can be whole. He spoke of the need for communities that can bridge the gap between "rich" and "poor" of all kinds and thus work towards uniting a divided world. I, along with everyone else present, was deeply touched by the simplicity and power of Vanier's message that so evidently flowed from the depths of his own heart. Here was a man with a profound love for people, especially the most down-trodden, a man with a thirst for peace and unity. He was evidently drawing much inspiration from the people with whom he had chosen to share his life.

Thus it was that when I went to Europe two years later I arranged to spend a month at l'Arche. How vividly I can recall that trip, beginning from the turmoil of the dingy North Station of Paris. The one-hour train ride to the north took me through the squalid suburbs and then through gentle farmland and charming villages clustered around magnificent little fifteenth and sixteenth century churches – scenes I had already admired in the paintings of the French Impressionists. Leaving the train at Compiègne, I again found myself in a city, but a city of forty thousand with nothing of the hustle and tumult of *gai Paris*. Someone was there to meet me, and to thus spare me waiting for the bus or the pain of trying to phone from the corner café to the constantly busy single telephone line at l'Arche. (They have since installed a switchboard, which has improved the situation only very slightly.) The warmth and joyful spirit of the woman who greeted me put me immediately at ease. Her disheveled appearance made it evident that clothes were one of her least concerns. She was obviously American but her manner of driving indicated that she had lived in France long enough to acquire the reckless abandon and agressivity that typifies the French way of handling a car – either like a toy or a lethal weapon. After fifteen breathless minutes of driving, during which she chatted and laughed like an old friend and I tried not to appear too stunned, we turned off the highway into the peaceful little village of Trosly, population nine hundred, nestled snugly against the beautiful Compiègne forest that rises around it on three sides. I noticed nothing special about this village because the community of l'Arche there simply occupies a scattered number of the old stone village houses. Soon, however, I found myself absorbed in what seemed like a completely other world.

During this month I spent my days in the workshop that does assembly work for a nearby plastic factory. It was not very complicated or challenging (just fit the red piece to the white piece and twist) but being there daily side-by-side with Raphael, Lucien, Jean-Luc, Norbert and the others, sharing in their lives, their frustrations and occasional crises, their love for music and laughter, their joy, their concern for others, their faith – all this was to make me more deeply aware of the truth of the words I had heard from the lips of Jean Vanier many months earlier. I was "hooked" on l'Arche.

So the following summer I found the time to join a group from l'Arche on one of their annual pilgrimages. This one was to Fatima. Here again, it was the simplicity of these people that impressed me most. It helped me to understand the meaning of Fatima and other such historical places where poor and simple children have been chosen to receive extraordinary graces and thus become messengers to thousands of others far more rich than they in human capacities and earthly goods. Subsequently, I spent a month of vacation in two consecutive summers at La Merci, a new community that l'Arche had begun in the Cognac region of France. While doing graduate studies in Spirituality at the Institut Catholique of Paris, I kept in close contact with l'Arche for a year and a half and then went there to live for the final year and a half of my stay in France.

My primary concern during these years of study in Europe was the question of community and, in particular, Christian community. I soon became aware that far more could be learned in this regard from a venture like l'Arche than from any amount of reading and discussion. So my interest turned more and more in this direction, and the openness and love of the people at l'Arche drew me more and more into the heart of its life.

I soon came to realize just what a unique community this is, not only with regard to its way of dealing with the problem of mental retardation but especially with regard to its response to critical issues that many people are facing today as individuals, families, and communities of all kinds. L'Arche, as it seems to me, is a much needed message for our times. It is a message that cannot be adequately translated into words, but it is a message of sufficient depth and importance that even a very inadequate translation can be of some significance. It is this latter conviction that gives me the courage to attempt this book, the aim of which is to enable others to experience this community and its message, at least in this vicarious way.

Jean Vanier's own words give us a first glimpse of just what the message of l'Arche is all about:

> More and more the world seems to be dividing itself into two. On the one hand there are those motivated by the accumulation of riches, by the need to possess, and by the need to dominate and be above others. On the other hand there are those who live in involuntary poverty and misery and who are in some way marginal to society (the aged, the handicapped of all

kinds, the alcoholics, the mentally ill, and so forth, and those who live in misery in the developing countries). Is not the great challenge of the day to create communities which by their joy and simplicity of life draw the "rich" towards a life of greater simplicity and self-gift, and that draw the miserable towards a new hope? Are not these new type of communities (which in fact are quite ancient since they resemble the first Christian communities) a great means of bringing a solution to the suffering, the war and the revolutions so prevalent in our times? When the distance between the society seeking domination and possession, and the miserable masses living in poverty becomes too great we can be sure that one day a spark will ignite the explosion. Do we not need communities of those who choose poverty, happy to share their lives with the rejected in order to create a bridge between the two worlds?

Joy and simplicity certainly do characterize the prevailing spirit of l'Arche. It was this spirit that first struck me upon arriving there. Visitors are almost invariably touched by this, and often they write letters of thanks that express something of what they have received there.

The mother of one of the assistants writes from Canada after having spent a week at l'Arche: "I find it very hard to put into words what is in my heart. My visit to your little village of Trosly will always remain one of the most rewarding experiences of my life."

The superior of a group of nuns who spent a weekend there writes: "The Sisters have absorbed there a climate of intelligent and total charity, of respect for others, that has done them an immense good."

A helicopter pilot in Korea writes to a friend he had visited briefly at l'Arche. It is interesting to note how, many months later, it is individual boys and assistants and even their expressions that remain dear to him:

> I got the very greatest news letter from Mr. Vanier last month. It touched my cold heart to read of the happy progress made at Trosly, and I took particular delight in remembering favourite names like René (of course), Bernard, le Père, Alain, Danielle, Michel, Abdullah – who was baptized at Carlepont. But what is the name of the philosopher, a champion, who said at Le Val Fleuri: "Un autre mort, merde!"

A seventeen year old lad from Amien, having passed several weeks at l'Arche writes:

> Having arrived home from my all too brief stay at Trosly I would like to express all the joy and contentment that I experienced there. It seems to

me that your community represents an oasis of joy and simplicity in our world.

These letters are merely typical of the comments made by the many visitors who pass through l'Arche. The final letter which I am going to cite at some length is rather less typical, not so much because of its contents, but rather because of the circumstances. The author had no previous knowledge of l'Arche but merely stopped there for a day and a half because a friend of his was there. He is a member of the Communist Party in Canada and an engineer by profession, who had a few months previously left his firm to come to Europe in search of some more meaningful way of life. After two fruitless months of searching he happened to stop at Trosly to visit his friend. A week after his departure he writes to his friend:

> After my hurried departure from the peaceful village of Trosly I felt a little ungrateful to have omitted thanking with words and gestures all those who made possible my stay in that veritable kingdom of Goodness and who each contributed in his own way to make it so pleasant for me . . . I only wish all of them could have read in the depths of my heart all the gratitude that I did not know how to express . . . I have lived at Trosly hours of interior peace that no sum of money could ever have gained for me . . . My stay in Frankfurt has been really most peaceful. I arrived there Friday noon and until my departure at eleven o'clock this morning I passed the major part of my time meditating and pondering over the experience I had lived out at Trosly. It is now several months since I left Montreal to escape the artificiality and to try to unearth in some corner of the world a little human warmth. I certainly never dreamed that I would have to traverse thousands of miles to have any chance of success and I was far from suspecting that in a little village of France perhaps not unlike villages in Quebec I would find the treasure I was seeking. As Jean Vanier said so well, the fellows of Trosly are "the superendowed with love." At Frankfurt I was trying to figure out how I could be one of them while at the same time assuming my responsibilities and accepting to be logical. Is this harmony possible? Will it finally fade away? The future will tell . . .

It was only after I had been there for several weeks that I began to realize that besides the joy, there is a tremendous amount of suffering that is also an essential element in the spirit of l'Arche. For many months this question of joy and suffering was brewing within me almost without my realizing it. Then one bright spring day at Trosly as I gazed out the window of my little room I saw something that suddenly illuminated this question and gave me a key to a better understanding of this community.

There in the garden beneath my window were two people at play, one a stunningly beautiful young woman, the other a severely handicapped man. L'Arche is in fact something just this simple as two people at play in a garden, but for all its simplicity it has a truly revolutionary message.

Myriam, a beautiful girl with much talent and a winning personality, chooses to spend her afternoons with Denis, who from all outward appearances possesses little that is attractive. Many would consider him to be repulsive in his sullenness, with his pursed features, and with not even enough awareness to blow his constantly running nose. Denis speaks very little, and when he does, they are usually words of violence. He has just come to l'Arche for a trial period. If all goes well he will come back on a permanent basis when there is room for him. His background evidently has been such as to create in him a very deep anguish and anger. Denis, like so many others, is the victim of a whole network and history of rejecting and aggressive actions. He has lived in a society that has made it impossible for his parents to simply love and accept him as the gift that he is, a society that in so many subtle and not so subtle ways has been telling him and those around him that he never should have been conceived, or at least he should have been destroyed while still in his mother's womb. Little wonder then that he is filled with fear, anguish and anger. So in some ways Myriam's role is to put a stop to this chain of violence, by responding to Denis' anguish not with a reaction of anger but with love and compassion. She is present to him as a source of peace that can draw out and absorb some of his anguish.

But she does not do this as a kind of stoic heroism. When I spoke later to Myriam about her relationship to Denis, she smiled gently and said how wonderful he is and how much she appreciated his company. Evidently, she had refused to be put off by his unattractive exterior, and had drawn close enough to perceive something of the inner riches of his person. This person she tries to call forth into greater fullness and vitality. It is an act of contemplation by which one is still and open enough to penetrate beyond the exterior of things to touch something of the hidden mystery of reality. Denis, on the other hand, in virtue of his very vulnerability and human poverty, calls Myriam forth into greater fullness and vitality. While he may threaten people who remain at a distance, Myriam has come close enough to sense the trembling and vulnerable person who is in such desperate need of her love. In the face of such a defenseless person she too can let down some of her own defenses and be much more open and transparent, much more her true self. In her relationship with Denis, Myriam is aware that each encounter can either call him forth to greater life, or leave him in or force him further into the death of loneliness and isolation. In this kind of relationship with the weak and defenseless we become aware of the way that all personal relationships are a matter of life and death. Thus at l'Arche there is an extraordinary opportunity to learn that each encounter with another person is an important moment — a moment in which to call the other forth, give him life, or in some way leave him in the death of his loneliness or self-doubt.

The challenge to the people of l'Arche to become sources of peace for one another gives birth to a twofold movement. On the one hand there is a movement towards interiority, towards deepening the well-springs of peace within oneself in order to be more of a source of peace for others. On the other hand, there is an outward movement towards the world steeped in violence and so much in need of men and communities of peace. Jean Vanier speaks of the need for a "revolution of love and compassion" to stem the tide of violence and division, and his community is, he hopes, a humble but real contribution to this revolution.

Vanier feels, and his community may indeed verify, that the peaceful revolution which alone can save mankind from destroying itself with the aggression of competition and the violence of self-defense is primarily an affair of the heart and an issue of community. Peace is, of course, the responsibility of all men, and perhaps especially of national and world leaders in the domains of politics, business, science and religion. However, these leaders are themselves caught in the dynamics of the power struggle of competition and defensiveness that leaves little hope for creative transformation. So the greatest hope is, perhaps, not in a transformation structured from without by political and economic measures or authoritative pronouncements but from within, by people who have experienced or at least sensed that there is an alternative to the path along which mankind is presently rushing towards self-destruction. Communities such as l'Arche, where the victims or "rejects" of society find the opportunity to be themselves and make their gift to the world, are living proof that there is an alternative.

The classic image of the beginning of man's separation from God and so from himself is the man and woman in the Garden of Eden refusing to accept their state of dependence. So we see as a kind of symbol of the revolution back towards unity a man and a woman at play in a garden. In Myriam and Denis there is the symbol of all that an individualistic and competitive society would claim as reasons for their having nothing to do with one another – the women's beauty and talent, the man's seeming lack of any beauty and talent. But Myriam and Denis (rich and poor, joy and suffering) are hand in hand as brother and sister. And they are at play – symbolic of freedom, of the going beyond death with childlike confidence in the Father and Lord of life.

L'Arche, as we shall see, is no Garden of Eden. The life is fraught with difficulties and much suffering. Many a person at Trosly or in the newer communities in France, India and North America, weighed down by some particular burden or simply by the dull monotony of the daily existence, is tempted to give it all up. Some, in fact, do just that. Others, however, are restored by the understanding eyes of a Raphael or an Isabel who, transcending their own frustrations of not being able to marry or not being able to speak, can with a mere look express so much love and compassion for a weary friend. Or they may be re-created, as I so often was by someone like my friend, Claude.

Claude has the most illogical mind that I have ever encountered so this may be the first and last time that he is ever quoted in a book. He may ask such questions as "What time is orange?" or "How was tomorrow"? but still he does have a wisdom all his own. As a result of his lack of logic he does many things wrong, so he suffers considerably from a kind of constant abuse which he has had to endure all his life. Yet Claude is marvelously resilient and keeps bouncing back joyfully. For those who discover his "music," his unique way of responding to life, he is a source of much joy. Well, one day Claude was at the beach with Jean-Pierre and several others of the Ambleteuse community. The ocean was at low tide so there was an immense stretch of flat, sandy beach. They began making designs in the sand. Claude drew a big circle with a couple of marks inside that could have been facial features. "What's that?" asked Jean-Pierre. With a big smile Claude replied: "It's Madame Sun." "That's good" Jean-Pierre said, "Now let's see you draw joy." Claude took a look around him at the wide beach that stretched out in both directions as far as the eye could see, then he turned to Jean-Pierre and said with a huge smile but in all seriousness: "There's not enough room!"

It is especially people like Claude, people who are deeply wounded, people who have been rejected by the world of "normality," who can speak a message of hope to that world. L'Arche is giving such people the chance to be themselves and make their contribution to society. While technological society with its values of competition and success is bordering on despair, communities of l'Arche are beginning to blossom forth. These communities, with their Claudes and their Isabels are telling us that there still is in this world enough room for joy, and they point the way to finding it.

Moments of attentiveness.

CHAPTER TWO

The Launching

O, Marie, nous vous demandons de bénir notre maison
Gardez-la dans votre coeur immaculé
Faites de l'Arche notre vrai foyer. . . .

We are at the evening prayer around the dinner table. The table has been cleared and the dishes washed. Three candles, spaced out on the long table, are presently the only source of light in the room. Their flickering light is enough to show the glowing faces of Raphael, Maxime, Jacques, Jean, Zizi, Benoit, Joan, Louise and a few of the others seated around the table. We number about fourteen tonight. The long, angular face of Jean Vanier radiates a deep peacefulness. Although only in his mid-forties, Vanier, by his ceaseless efforts and concern for others, has taken on the appearance of a much older man – a man of wisdom.

Many had been at the community Mass earlier this evening. I know Maxime was there, as I saw him still in the chapel sometime after the Mass. He always remains to make his thanksgiving, during which time, as he says, he sings canticles in his heart to express his gratitude and he listens to Jesus who speaks to him in his heart. I had concelebrated the Mass with Père Thomas, the saintly Dominican priest that l'Arche is fortunate to have as its chaplain. The sermon of this retired philosophy professor betrayed only a little of his Thomistic background. They were words to satisfy the most intelligent minds and the most profound spirits, but words delivered with a warmth and simplicity that held the attention of even the most handicapped listeners.

As I step outside from this very modest but oddly charming and prayerful chapel and close the door behind me, there is only the cross on the door to distinguish it from the other gray stone village houses.

Now in early November it is already dark at seven in the evening. Across the village square I can just make out the form of what used to be the town's only hotel. It is now la Source, one of the homes of l'Arche. I can hear Maxime moving quickly away down the street. It is too dark to see him, but I recognize the dragging foot of his paralyzed right side, and the enthusiastic, if not too melodious singing that expresses something of his inner joy. I follow him down the street past the *bistro* where some of the men of the village are gathered for their evening chat over a few glasses of wine, and past the little stone houses which have been standing here for centuries. Their closed shutters hide the simple and hardy people who are now beginning their evening meal. A couple of the houses seem more familiar to me. Here, Madame Cagniard lives with her son and daughter-in-law. She does the laundry in the Val Fleuri and her daughter-in-law does most of the housecleaning. There is the Pigeonnier where eight or ten of the women assistants room, and next to it the Sénevé which houses five or six more.

Finally, I catch up with Maxime. He extends his uncrippled left hand in greeting and gives me a big smile: "Bonsoir, mon Père." While we exchange a few words Maxime continues humming and singing. After the Mass he just cannot contain his joy. So together we arrive at the little house at the end of the street. The wooden plaque over the door is just visible thanks to the welcoming lamp at the door: "l'Arche."

As we step inside from the cold November evening, we are greeted by the warmth, the light, the smell of good cooking, and the joyful voices, all of which blends into the overall impression of "home." I join those who are relaxing in the living room. Roger is enjoying a cigarette. Jim is reading, as usual. Benoit is in front of the radio, bouncing up and down in time with the music. Zizi is writing and conferring with Pierrot for the next issue of the Trosly-Potin, l'Arche's weekly newspaper (4 or 5 mimeograph pages, circulation of 85, price 10 centimes). Judging from their laughter, it is not going to be a very serious edition this week, which will surprise no one. Joan is knitting. Raphael comes in, gives me a big smile, and begins mumbling and gesticulating. While I am trying to decipher his message, Louise, in the other room begins to ring a little cow bell, and calls:

"*à table.*" The readiness with which we begin moving through the little hallway into the dining room indicates how hungry we are. The volume of talking and laughing mounts steadily as others arrive from their rooms upstairs or come in the front door which opens on the dining room. The decor of the house is very simple: stone tile floors, no rugs, some photos and pictures hanging on the papered walls, cheap but colourful printed drapes on the windows. An oil stove heats the living room, and another the dining room.

We find our places around the table by finding the napkin ring with our name. A simple process since the places usually don't vary that much. The paper napkins are for the guests. There are several this evening, invited from the other houses, which swells our number to over twenty. It is quite crowded but no one seems to mind. Everyone is obviously used to this·sort of thing.

Jean Vanier's place in the middle is presently vacant, which indicates that he will arrive soon. Louise hands the Bible to Jacques. He leafs through it searching for a text. The room becomes a bit quieter. Pierrot continues to banter Philippe, and Raphael is still trying to tell me something by repeating in his mumbling way something that sounds like "*pas-là.*" Then Jacques makes the sign of the cross and others follow suit. In his boyish voice Jacques reads a brief passage of the Gospel, flawlessly pronouncing each word and phrase. Silence for an instant and then Pierrot begins singing a grace. We all join in enthusiastically. By the last phrase most of us have gotten the right key. The scraping of chairs and everyone sits down, and Louise begins serving up the steaming soup. The bantering and laughing picks up immediately. Three or four conversations are going all at once. Raphael again tries to get through to me: "pas là." "Who is not here?" I ask, and he points to himself with an almost violent gesture and grunts what I have come to recognize as the word "moi." So Raphael will not be here, but when? More gestures and mumbling which I can't understand. But Lulu, who has been here almost as long as Raphael and the other "founding fathers," Pierrot and Philippe, is there to help. After a couple of guesses he says: "Saturday," and Raphael smiles and nods in agreement. "But where are you going?" I continue, and he gives me a military salute. Now I'm distracted as Veronique at my left asks me if I can reach the soup and serve up another bowl to Jacques. Then a couple of others pass their soup plates. Finally, turning back to Raphael, I see that he is now trying to explain the same message to Barbara.

I can now be of some help, since I've deciphered the first half of the message: "he says he won't be here to eat on Saturday." And now Raphael nods and begins to salute again. "You're going to visit your friend, the army chaplain?" I suggest, but it is not that. "You're going to do your military service," someone suggests but he shakes his head. Then Barbara who, although she is a guest in our home this evening has known Raphael since her arrival at Trosly shortly after l'Arche was begun, says: "It's Camille, the brother of Anne-Marie." Anne-Marie, a girl of the village, does the cooking at l'Arche. Her brother Camille is doing his military service. Raphael is one great smile as he nods in assent. "Anne-Marie has invited you to eat with them Saturday evening?" Barbara continues. Raphael finally relaxes back in his chair and smiles with contentment, giving us all a look that says: "It was perfectly obvious what I was trying to say, what took you so long to understnad."

Meanwhile Pierrot has been at his favourite pastime of kidding Zizi. Although he claims to have had his fill of Canadians he gets along famously with this young French Canadian who is taking a year off from her studies to work at l'Arche. "Sha ta"he says, trying out some of his newly-learned English, with a big toothy grin. We have come to recognize this expression which is supposed to be "shut up."

The front door opens, and the tall figure of Vanier steps quietly into the room. He is slightly stooped from years of bending to give his full attention to smaller people. He smiles and bows in a gesture of humble apology. A clatter of happy voices go up in mock protest.

Raphael grunts what we all know to be the words "Too late! Too late!" Pierrot exclaims: "No excuses! No excuses!" While Marie-Elizabeth quickly goes to the kitchen for some hot soup. Vanier takes his place at the table, manifesting great contentment to be with his family. Simply and unpretentiously he turns all his attention now to Jacques, now to Benoit, to George, Louise and so on, calling forth each of them to be more a part of the entire gathering.

Thus the meal proceeds in a very cheerful atmosphere. Most people seem very much at home, but some, like George, are very quiet and exchange only a few whispered words with their neighbour. Benoit responds mechanically and very briefly to questions that are put to him, but is otherwise occupied with his food and his own thoughts which sometimes cause him to smile broadly or other times to strike himself sharply on the cheek. At the end of each course in the meal, a few people get up without a word being said. They take out the soup pot or serving dishes, as the case may be, and bring in the next course.

Several baskets of fruit are brought in for dessert. Someone has put the plastic banana in with the oranges and pears. Most of us spot it immediately and exchange knowing smiles. The basket is offered to Philippe, who loves bananas. He reaches quickly for his favourite fruit but as soon as he touches it he knows he has been "had." "*Merde*," he shouts, and everyone bursts into laughter, especially Raphael, who all but falls off his chair, which provokes even more laughter.

When the meal is finally finished we all stand and join in as Pierrot begins a rousing song of thanksgiving.

There is a race for the kitchen to see who will get to the sink first and thus wash the dishes. Vanier quickly stretches out his long arm and holds back Marie-Elizabeth in order to step in front of her. But Veronique is closer to the door leading towards the kitchen. Vanier races after her. As Veronique goes around the kitchen table which blocks the way to the sink, Vanier leaps over it and lands at the sink before her.

Veronique screams with excitement and the shock of almost being trapped under this immense form descending from above. Vanier bursts into laughter as he roles up his sleeves and fills the sink. Everyone helps to clear the table and do the dishes. Jacques rinses, and Raphael hands the dishes to be dried to those waiting patiently or not so patiently with their dish towels. It would go much quicker if Raphael were not there, but each time he hands out a dripping plate it is accompanied by such a look of friendship, that no one regrets the extra few minutes. The little kitchen is a scene of happy chaos.

Soon the dishes are finished and most of us return to the dining room for the evening prayer. As usual, Philippe suggests that we don't delay too long with the prayer so that he won't miss the start of the film or whatever the program happens to be on the TV. This evening, at the request of Vanier, Maxime leads the prayer. He begins by asking if anyone has any particular intentions. Pierre beside me has just whispered that he is very sad in thinking of his mother who died last year, and his father who died the year before. It is the day following All Souls Day. I suggest that we pray for Pierre and his departed parents. After a moment's silence, Jacques takes this up, and speaks of how he felt when he was very young and his parents died. He says something to the effect that: "It was extremely hard, and I didn't want to believe it when they told me my mother had died, and I refused to go and look at her corpse." After a pause he continues: "Yes, it's tough at the beginning, but you sooner or later get accustomed to it – and they are happy in heaven, and that's the most important thing."

This time of prayer is a very privileged moment of truth, when people will express their deepest feelings, feelings they would never dare to express in another context. Like the evening when each one was saying what aspect of Jesus and his life meant most to us, and Pierrot said that, for him, it was how Jesus gave sight to the blind man. Then he continued by telling us that his own father was losing his eyesight.

So now Jacques invites Maxime to speak: "And you, Maxime, do you have any intentions?" Maxime suggests that we pray for Gabrielle and Ron who are in India. Yes, says Jacques, and especially for those poor and lonely people who will come and find refuge at Asha Niketan. Then Joan, a Toronto girl who has been at l'Arche since the summer, says in her less than perfect French, that we could pray for Regina who will be leaving Thursday to join the others in India. Silence. Then Bruno, who is always up on current events, says something about the youth recently killed in a dance hall fire in southern France, suggesting that we pray for those who have died and for their families. Quietly Vanier begins to speak of his concern for one of the newly-established homes elsewhere in France. The young couple in charge feel very fragile and in need of the support of our prayers. Then, in great simplicity, he speaks to Jesus in a way that makes us all feel very much the presence of his unseen friend.

A long silence, and then Pierrot begins singing the Our Father and all join in. Raphael, too, with undistinguishable sounds and no recognizable tune, adds what he can to the singing. It is followed immediately by the l'Arche prayer:

O Marie, nous vous demandons . . .
Mary, we ask you to bless our house.
Keep it safe in your immaculate heart.
Make l'Arche our true home –
A refuge for the poor in spirit
That they may find here the Source of all life –
A refuge for those who are severely tried
That they may be ceaselessly consoled.
Mary, give us hearts that are humble and gentle

28

To welcome with kindness and compassion
All those whom you send to us.
Give us hearts full of mercy
To love them, to serve them, to extinguish all discord
And to see in our suffering brother the living presence of Jesus.
Lord, bless us from the hand of your poor.
Lord, smile on us through the eyes of your poor.
Lord, receive us one day in the holy company of your poor.
Amen.

Then Pierrot whispers: "Notre-Dame de l'Arche, priez pour nous!"
(Our Lady of l'Arche, pray for us!) to which all respond quietly:
"Amen." "Notre-Dame de Lourdes, priez pour nous!" "Amen."
Maxime continues: "Notre-Dame del 'Inde, priez pour nous!"
"Amen." Notre-Dame de l'Aurore (for Daybreak in Canada), priez
pour nous!" "Amen." "Notre-Dame de la paix, priez pour nous!"
"Amen." Silence, and then Pierrot begins a hymn to the Blessed
Virgin and all join in, including Raphael. Finally, there is a silence
that envelops everyone. The candles flicker in the darkness. A profound sense of peace and unity pervades the room. It holds us all
breathlessly still for a couple of minutes, then Maxime makes the sign
of the cross. Others follow. Jacques leans over the table to blow out
the candles, and Zizi tries to blow them out before he can. Someone
turns on the lights. Raphael, getting to his feet, drops his pipe, which
evokes the one word he can say with perfect clarity: "*Merde*."

Vanier begins saying goodnight to each one, taking their hand and
looking intently and lovingly into their eyes. A few people move into
the living room to relax, listen to records, read or write letters. Pierre
challenges Roger to a chess match. Raphael comes to me and asks if I
will perform the wedding ceremony for himself and whatever girl
happens to be nearby. Tonight it's Joan. This being Tuesday, Maxime gets his coat to return to the chapel. A couple of others, after
saying goodnight and shaking hands with everyone, slip out and head
for the chapel. Lulu is already in his room listening to the records.
The sounds of a Bach Organ Recital are wafted down the stairs.

Vanier soon catches up with Philippe, takes him by the arm and
proceeds down the road with him. Vanier is going to his office, where
until late into the night he will be engaged with some paper work, but
mostly with members of the community, who will come to see him on
business or for personal guidance.

So the evening draws to an end peacefully, as they generally have since Jean Vanier settled here at l'Arche some eight years ago. A vaguely similar evening has been spent in the other homes that have been opened in Trosly in the intervening years.

Perhaps, peaceful would not be the word to describe the Val Fleuri. It is the largest of the homes, in fact, with some thirty-five handicapped and eight assistants, it is almost too large to be called a home. However, anyone assisting at a meal in this great old chateau could not help but be touched by the warmth and joyfulness of the atmosphere. The Val Fleuri is actually where it all began.

In 1960, Mr. Pratt, the father of a mentally handicapped boy, and Dr. Préaut, with many years of professional experience with the handicapped, began the Val Fleuri, as a residence and workshop for mentally handicapped young men. They invited Père Thomas Philippe to come to Trosly as the chaplain because they wanted this home to have a religious orientation. As Père Thomas reflects, these two men invited him to come precisely as a chaplain, "as a poor instrument who could help individuals live more fully in the Holy Spirit." It was very clear right from the beginning, he notes, that here at Trosly there would be given this special orientation of helping each person to develop an interior life, more and more illuminated and guided by the Holy Spirit.

A year later, at the urging of Père Thomas, his friend and former tutor, Jean Vanier, comes to Trosly. It marks for him the end of a long search, and the beginning of an extraordinary and, at that time, unsuspected career.

Jean Vanier, was born in 1928, the son of Pauline and the late General George Vanier, a distinguished soldier and later Governor General of Canada. Jean seemed destined, from a very early age, to follow his father in a military career. Robert Speaight notes, in his biography of General Vanier, that in 1942:

> Jock (as Jean is called by his family) had passed into the Royal Naval College, Dartmouth, now removed to Eaton Hall in Cheshire. A report described him as having no great gifts in the way of brains or athletic ability, but he is a very likeable character and should do well in the long run. In view of his subsequent achievements this was an understatement wholly in keeping with the traditions of the Royal Navy. (p.256)

At the age of twenty, Jean is already an officer on Canada's only aircraft carrier. His mother remembers the response of her husband to a report sent to the General concerning his son some years earlier when he was a student at Dartmouth. The report noted that Jean showed some good qualities for an officer but that he lacked respect for his senior officers. "As long as he never shows a lack of respect for those under him, he'll be all right," the General responded happily. At that time, of course, he had no idea of the great respect and concern that his son was to acquire for the weakest and most defenseless members of society.

The Lord soon indicated to Jean that He had other things in mind for him than the concerns of an aircraft carrier. (This ship has recently been sold for scrap, while Vanier's fragile little Ark shows signs of staying afloat for some time to come.) Vanier reflects that when he found himself reciting the divine office instead of attending to the night watch it became rather evident that the navy was not his place. So in 1950 he resigned his commission with the Royal Canadian Navy.

Thus began a long period of searching. He made enquiries into several different lay communities that in one way or another were concerned with living the Gospel in a spirit of poverty. One such community of which he had some slight knowledge, was Eau Vive in France. The response to his enquiry about this community, a letter from its founder and director Père Thomas Philippe, convinced him to go there, in preference to several other interesting possibilities. This was a community of students, located in a poor suburb of Paris, next to the Dominican Priory of the Sauchoir. Its purpose was to give to its members a deeper commitment to their Christian faith by training them in prayer and metaphysics. At the time of Vanier's arrival it consisted of about 80 students. A year later, ill health forced Père Thomas to give up the direction of Eau Vive. It is an indication of the respect that Père Thomas had for Vanier that he should hand over the direction to him, after only one year's acquaintance with this former naval officer who is some twelve years junior to him.

This change in leadership precipitated a crisis in Eau Vive's relationship with the Sauchoir. The Dominicans had considered Eau Vive to be under their jurisdiction, and so were unhappy that its direction should be taken over by a layman. The doors of the Sauchoir were closed to the members of Eau Vive. Being denied the opportunity of studying with the Dominicans and the use of their library, many students left Eau Vive, dropping its number to about twenty-five. Most of those who remained, pursued their studies at the

Institut Catholique in Paris. Eau Vive managed to survive this crisis and continue for six or seven years.

Meanwhile, Jean Vanier had been accepted as a candidate to the priesthood for the diocese of Quebec, with the blessing of the bishop to continue his studies in Europe. Just shortly before he was to return to Quebec to prepare for the subdiaconate, a new crisis arose at Eau Vive, of which he was still the director. The local bishop was forced to ask Vanier and other leaders to resign and to sign a statement of submission to Church authority. Vanier recalls that the Bishop was embarrassed to the point of confusion. So much that he accidentally handed Vanier the wrong statement, namely, a declaration of refusal to submit to the Church.

We might just note a recent event which is in striking contrast to this episode of a decade ago. The ten thousand people who happened to be in St. Peter's Basilica for the Wednesday audience prior to Pentecost of this present year, have no doubt that Vanier is a loyal son of the Church. Vanier was there that day with some two hundred members of the communities from Trosly and La Merci on pilgrimage to the eternal city. As he went up on the dais and was presented to Paul VI, the two men warmly embraced each other in a sign of mutual love and respect.

In any case, the dismissal from Eau Vive left Vanier in a state of uncertainty not unlike that of seven years previous to this when he resigned from the Navy. He decided against entering the major seminary to complete his final year of preparation for the priesthood.

The next few years were lived with little or no experience of community. They include a year boarding at the Trappist monastery of Bellefontaine. Another year was spent on a small farm he purchased and where, in his own words, he "lived very much alone." During a year spent in Rome he continued some private studies in theology with his friend, Père Thomas. One of the last of these years of search was spent in a little cottage at Fatima which he had purchased some years earlier in the hope that it might be the location for a new community of Eau Vive. In 1962 he successfully defended his doctorate in philosophy at the Institut Catholique in Paris, and then joined the faculty of St. Michael's College, University of Toronto, to begin a part-time teaching career which he has never totally abandoned.

That same year, Père Thomas had begun as the chaplain of Val Fleuri. A year later, encouraged by Père Thomas, Jean came to

Trosly where he bought the dilapidated, old house which was christened l'Arche and set afloat on August 5, 1964.

Looking back on the years that preceded the founding of l'Arche, Jean Vanier feels that his six years in the community of Eau Vive were the "most formative of these long years of searching – even far more than the actual studies pursued." In any case, he had come to the conviction that he was called to form community, and this with some of the poor and rejected of society. Jean says that in moving into his little house with Raphael and Philippe, he was sure of only one thing. In taking these men out of the institutions to which they had been condemned and bringing them to l'Arche, he was making an irrevocable move. He had no idea whether there would be other people willing to come and help him, but he did know that he was committed to live with these men for the rest of his life or theirs.

His decision caused considerable consternation among his family and friends who could not understand this sacrifice of a most promising career in the University for a seemingly worthless alternative. However, Vanier knew that this was something he had to do in response to a call that was too clear to deny or ignore.

The ten-year search for community had thus terminated in his commitment to share his life with two lonely and rejected men. There was no glamour and no clear plan or vision for the future in moving into this ramshackled house in an out-of-the-way corner of the world. This simple, concrete gesture was the thing at hand to be done, and Vanier did it. It was this gesture that sowed the seed for all that is now flourishing out of Vanier's inspiration, like a fulfilment of the words of the Gospel: "Unless a grain of wheat falls into the ground and dies, it remains alone; but if it dies, it bears much fruit." (Jn 12:24)

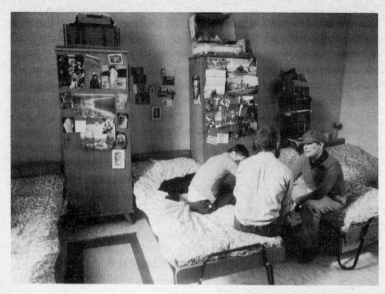

At home at Val Fleuri:
sharing problems *(top)*;
greeting the new day *(right)*.

At work: in the pottery shop (*top*); in the garden.

"Everybody needs a grandmother." — Madame Vanier.

CHAPTER THREE

Setting The Course

L'Arche has taken on dimensions far beyond the expectations held by Jean Vanier when he began his little home in the summer of '64. He says that his original idea was to create "a home of mercy where the rejects of society could find refuge and where they would be welcomed with kindness and compassion." However, after a month or two living with Raphael and Philippe he began to formulate a quite different vision.

Out of the commitment to live with the handicapped came the discovery of their gifts and potential. Vanier noticed, for example, how Philippe was making a slide collection with which to entertain his friends. Raphael would save the many matches he used each day in lighting his pipe. These he would take for a little boy down the street to play with. He would hide away chocolates and other such gifts that he might share them with others. Before long he had become the friend of many in the village, especially with the children and the elderly who found no problem with Raphael's almost complete inability to speak. These men had both the need and the capacity to give to others. Vanier came to realize that "if the handicapped are given a good human situation in which to live and are sustained by loving relationships, they are capable of progressing in an astonishing way on the psychological, human and spiritual planes."

Along with this discovery came an event which also widened the scope of l'Arche. Three months after Vanier had settled in the town of Trosly there was a crisis in the direction of the Val Fleuri. The Val Fleuri comprised a large residence (the old village chateau) and pro-

37

tected workshops (the chateau stables) for about twenty mentally handicapped young men. Vanier was asked to take over its direction. A doctorate in philosophy had scarcely prepared him for such a venture, but under the strong encouragement of Père Thomas he accepted the position.

He can now laugh at the way he practiced on an orange before giving his first hypodermic needle to a very agitated young man. Besides learning how to treat and give other immediate help to these people, he was also learning about the nature of their suffering. As he says: "Since their infancy almost all the handicapped have been wounded not only organically but by so many looks of pity, disdain and indifference that have made them feel worthless and inferior and have destroyed any confidence they may have had in themselves." So what they most needed was to be loved and accepted as people.

Others were needed who would be willing to come and live with the handicapped on this level of acceptance and friendship. They began to come in response to Vanier's invitation as he spoke of his work to people in France, and in Canada where he continued to lecture on a part-time basis. There were people like Henri, from the North of France, and Barbara, from Buffalo, who came and are still there. Others like Steve and Anne, and Agnes and Adriano came for a while and then moved on to start other l'Arche communities. Many came for the summer months or longer periods as a break from studies or other work. Those who came also quickly began to discover the riches of Raphael, Philippe and the others. Anne-Marie, a student from Quebec, observed: "Raphael brings me so much – his smile is extraordinary." David a college graduate from Ontario took a while but finally discovered Raphael:

> He's such a genuine person. I couldn't understand this until last Saturday when I went to say goodbye to everybody. I walked out to my car, and Raphael was standing over near the fence just a bit from my car. So I went over to say goodbye to him and explain to him that I was leaving – and all of a sudden – just the look in his eyes, the sadness, the real feeling of genuine sadness. He said: "*pas pars,*" you can't leave, you have to stay and work. Just a simple statement, but for me at the point it was just too much. That was the first time that I felt that I had communicated with him. And just to watch his eyes then. I understand now what people mean because he has such an open spirit, he accepts people so beautifully. There's a communication problem. too. You have to know Raphael pretty well in order to be able to communicate with him. It took me quite a while

to beam in on his sort of communication. The other night I was back there to see Mary and Judy and he was standing outside Mary and Judy's room. And he turned to his right and saw these flowers that were blooming on a bush, and he said they were very beautiful: *"Ils poussent bien."* And then he turned to his left and there were some of those little snowdrop flowers and they were all dead. And you could just see the change in his eyes from the joy when he looked at the live flowers to the sadness when he saw the dead ones. It was beautiful.

While people came with many different motives almost invariably they were surprised at how much they received, especially from the handicapped. For Diane and Helen, "It was just a way to pass the summer." Yet to their delight, "It has been a very, very beautiful experience – we had such terrific friends among the boys."*

Tom, a school teacher reflects: "I don't think I had any particularly humanitarian motives . . . I was interested and now I'm even more interested." He concludes: "It's like living in a very big family – which is great." Dave, a graduate student in theology, observes: "Really you come here thinking you want to serve, help out where you can, but you get more out of it than you can possibly give."

Pierre came from a nearby city in France. He had a clear idea of

* Note: it is important to try and clarify the use of this term "boys". It is the most common way of referring to the mentally handicapped men at l'Arche. We must realize, however, that the youngest there is eighteen, and, although the majority are in their early twenties, there is no upper age limit. At present the oldest, Raphael, is forty-six. On several occasions, in reunions of assistants, many of the assistants have indicated that they are not too happy with this term, boys (*garçons*). However, no one has been able to suggest a more satisfying term. The dissatisfaction is due to the fact that the term "boys," is too paternalistic and suggests that there is a failure to sufficiently respect the handicapped for the men that they are. Yet, the suggested options, *les hommes*, *les pensionnaires*, *les patients*, and so forth, all seem to suggest an institution, such as a prison or hospital, and seem to accentuate the separation between the assisted and the assisting, which separation they are trying to reduce to a minimum. So they have been left with the term boys. The term, however, is used more in the sense that we would speak of the boys or the fellows on a football team or in a college dorm, rather than as to the children in opposition to the adults. The problem is also partly linguistic. In the communities that have since begun in English-speaking countries the handicapped adults are referred to as the men and women, and not *"les garçons"* and *"les filles,"* as in France.

why he came there: "I came first of all because I plan to go into the profession of special education, and secondly to experience real community life." He goes on to say: "I think the boys have given me much more than I expected." Anne-Marie, a college girl from Montreal, says: "I was afraid I wouldn't be able to accept this kind of person, but I discovered that they are great – they humanize us a great deal."

As people came and were so obviously enriched by living with the handicapped it became more and more evident that l'Arche was not just a place of refuge. It was a community where all could progress together towards greater wholeness. If it was not to be simply a refuge, neither was it just a place to do nothing but try and be a community. For one thing, there was work to be done. There were the workshops and gardens as well as the maintenance and daily chores of the homes. However, both the work and the community life itself is at the service of the growth and development of the individual. As Vanier sees it: "The aim of this community is not efficiency and productivity, but human and spiritual progress, which ought necessarily to be founded on an openness and mutual respect, and the desire to see the other achieve the greatest possible liberty."

This greater liberty, the freedom to be more oneself, was certainly being experienced by many. The very simplicity of the handicapped seems to be a key to open others and allow them to be more simple and more truly themselves.

Mary, a nurse, claimed: "I could be myself at l'Arche – yes, very much, because one is not threatened, and there is such welcome. They really accept you and make you feel at home." Tom finds his own self more, thanks to the simplicity he met in the handicapped:

> I think it's the simplicity of the boys. There's no need of doing a lot – you can't distract them anyway. The relationship that exists between ourselves and the boys is so simple. They don't want a whole bunch of talk, or that you buy anything for them. They're not interested in how bright you are, what degrees you have, what kind of clothes you wear. All that they want to do is to take your hand, or have you put your arm around their shoulder, or tell them they're doing a good job, or horse around with them. They don't look for anything but the essentials. When they can't verbalize, when they can't speak very well, they don't know enough to have all the damn stupid hang-ups we've got. It's just real simple.

Judy, a pre-med student, also speaks of the matter of people being themselves, and of accepting people as they are:

40

L'Arche is such a sincere place. People can be themselves, and it doesn't matter what you were at home, or where you come from, or what degrees you have. I think all the people here, all the Canadians have changed – I know I have, in small ways, I know I have very much. And you think now of the people at home, and some of the things that you hear at home, some of the standards that are set, the standards on which you judge people, and they are so meaningless now. All that's important is the type of person you are and the type of rapport you can establish with the boys and whether you are sincere or not, On the surface it's a way of looking at people, as they are and not as people say they are. Still there is something more than this, something deeper. It's largely because of l'Arche that the boys are so rich in spirit. I've met other mentally handicapped people – they have had the same quality, but it's so much brought out at l'Arche. There's always been the same simplicity but there's never been the same richness. Like when you go to the beach and you see Jean-Claude, and René acting up. There's no pretence to them at all, They're real people. They are more real than so many other people I know, who are supposed to have everything. That struck me the first time I saw them in public – it was fantastic. That's what's so wonderful. I don't know if I can – if people can – just be themselves. Not be embarrassed or shy or anything.

The various façades that people use to hide behind are much less effective with simple people. They have a way of seeing the person behind the façade, and of relating directly to that person. They are especially sensitive to the suffering of others. It is a common experience at l'Arche for one of the fellows to offer compassion by a look, or a word or gesture to someone whose suffering is scarcely observable. There was, for example, André who spent a few weeks at l'Arche after leaving the monastery where he had lived for a number of years. Few people knew that he was an ex-monk, and even fewer people knew of his deep suffering because he was always laughing. One night at the evening prayer at the Val Fleuri, Patrick, a marvellous little man who is quite markedly mongoloid, said: "Let us pray for André because he is not very happy." He went on to say how very sorry he felt for André.

Vanier stated that the aim of l'Arche is not efficiency and productivity. He had been learning from these people another alternative to the excessive emphasis that Western society places on efficiency and productivity. It is especially the North Americans who come to l'Arche that are struck by the way other values precede those of efficiency and productivity. They all speak of how "the pace of life has slowed down" so that life has become more enjoyable. Linked with this is the fact that, "there isn't this pressure to accomplish things, concrete things," but rather more concern is given to the people who are doing the job than the job itself. Judy illustrates this very well: "It's when Raphael wants to help with the potatoes that have to be done by four o'clock; so Raphael helps and they're not done until four-thirty and they're done horribly." Thomas gives an example of how his own attitude has changed in this regard:

> I'll never forget this one thing. We were digging a hole, and it was full of water, and the guy I was working with, Michael, was throwing the water out with a bucket – the most inefficient way of doing it – but he was laughing because the muddy water was splashing up on the trees and the sun was shining through it and it was really pretty, it really looked neat. We just stood there and watched it for about five minutes, and it was really great. That was towards the end of the summer. I would not have enjoyed it at the beginning of the summer because, well, all that water and the hole that we had to get dug. But it was little simple things like that.

There is this stress upon the present moment, enjoying it without being too preoccupied about the future, and so gaining a deeper appreciation for what the moment holds: "just enjoying the afternoon without worrying about what's going to happen tonight and . . . getting things done at the same time, and enjoying everyone around you." So there is this greater appreciation not just of people but also of nature as Thomas' example indicates, and as he goes on to say:

> You appreciate little things more, too, just little things of beauty. I notice myself looking at flowers more, and sunsets. Although I always did like that sort of thing, they've become more important.

David adds to this how he has gained a deeper appreciation for the basic aspects of life:

> I feel in a sort of undefined way that the definitions for some of the very basic aspects of life have been shaken up or, you know, something like that. What sleep means and what work means and what eating means – it's not what I knew before, and I feel that it's more meaningful. I feel richer in that because I have lived, worked, slept and eaten with the boys.

One aspect of the life-style of l'Arche which until now has been referred to only indirectly is the means of communication between people. Here I am not referring to the passing on of information or instructions but simply of interpersonal communication. This, of course, has been implied in what has been said about a greater appreciation for others and a greater openness. Also, it was mentioned how "the boys are uninhibited" in expressing their affections even sometimes to the point of "handling you and kissing you and that sort of thing," as one person remarks. Or, as Judy explains: "I think it's fantastic, when I can go downstairs and the boys will be there and they will take you into their arms almost."

But touch is not the only non-verbal communication that is emphasized here. Francoise speaks of the importance of silence itself as a means of personal encounter: "I find that the silence is really extraordinary – it's true – people meet one another much more profoundly in silence." She goes on to say how much can be communicated simply by a smile:

In the workshop there are moments when no one is talking and we are really united. Even by a smile I find that the smile is very, very important. There is no need for words, but to smile at a boy – you touch him much more – it's extraordinary – it's really true. Take Patrick, for example, nothing but a smile, but when he smiles he seems to say: "You know, I really love you." There is something extraordinary there, and nothing has been said. It's extraordinary . . . Raphael doesn't speak very much, but just the same there are things quite profound that happen . . . Raphael has a good gimmick, he's unable to speak.

The openness of simple people also operates on the level of faith, making possible a very simple and direct relationship with God. Many at l'Arche relate to Jesus as to a personal and intimate friend. Prayer and worship is very important to them, which rather surprises many of the more sophisticated people who come there. Like Donald, a theology student, who spent a summer at l'Arche. He says:

That was one of the big things that struck me – why the boys were always going to Mass when they were perfectly free to go or not. It was just like a big circus, all that racket and noise – and as I went on, I began to realize that for most of the boys Mass is a meaningful experience . . . Even for Patrick D, the innocent of innocents. It's his best quality. He's incapable of wrong in the moral sense. There is that spiritual part and this has come out from time to time. One time when it came out was when we were having one of those prayer meetings Sunday evening – everyone was sort of surprised – he just sort of took over. Even for him there's this very spiritual force working but it's not that apparent half the time, but it's apparent that there is some spiritual meaning in the Mass and prayers for him. Another thing that I really liked was the little prayer after dinner. It was kept short, seven to ten minutes, and yet the boys seemed to really enjoy it.

For some, like Brian, this simple faith effected a kind of conversion experience, as he says:

I had kind of forgotten about God. Then, almost without realizing it, here his presence overwhelmed me and it's almost like coming back to the fold – because where I wanted to question and everything I realized that it was beyond questioning here and that He was a very real Person because there was nothing else that could make something like this work. And as such I've recognized it in people and what they do – their desire to pray. Because of His overwhelming presence here it refreshed my mind when it was on the breach of stalemate. Something that sort of struck me with the boys is that – well, young adults always like to question the existence of God and theology and different religions and see what is best for them. Then to see the boys here who just believe. It's almost like blind faith – it's fantastic – it's beyond questioning. They just accept it and live within it. That is also something that struck me very strongly: this recognition of Christ – when I say Christ I mean the presence of God.

We can at this point simply sum up the various qualities of the men at l'Arche that have been spoken of as a source of inspiration: simplicity of spirit; affection and freedom to genuinely manifest this affection; candidness; openness to life, to people, to God; capacity to make people feel welcome; tendency to be concerned only with the essentials in life and in people; joy and an eagerness to give joy to others; generosity; capacity to live fully the present moment; sense of wonder; sensitivity; unquestioning faith. These are qualities which can be most readily attributed to the child, but they are, nevertheless, very positive attributes. Clearly, the people who have come to l'Arche feel that they have been influenced in a very positive way by their contact with the boys. It has not been simply the experience of serving poor and helpless creatures that they have found to be so personally enriching, but rather the interpersonal relations with fellow human beings who have much to offer.

This is really not the time and place for analysis but I cannot resist the temptation to draw into the conversation a psychologist of human relations who might help us to understand what is at issue here. Eric Berne in his *Games People Play* points out that in every person there is the Child, the Adult and the Parent. He goes on to note that: "there is no such thing as an 'immature person' – there are only people in whom the Child takes over inappropriately or unproductively."

While noting the importance of the Adult for the survival of the individual and of the Parent for both the survival of the human race, and the conservation of much time and energy by making many responses automatic, he nevertheless stresses the importance of the Child to "contribute to the individual's life exactly what an actual child can contribute to family life: charm, pleasure and creativity."

The major part of Berne's study is given to the analysis of the various kinds of games people play as a means of social intercourse that circumvents the threatening relationship of intimacy. Intimacy is the richest form of human relation, but few people have enough personal autonomy to engage in such relations. The natural Child possesses this autonomy, but rarely does he resist the parental influence which tends to destroy it. "The attainment of autonomy," he notes, "is manifested by the release or recovery of three capacities: awareness, spontaneity and intimacy."

Spontaneity, as Berne defines it, means, "liberation, liberation from the compulsion to play games and have only the feelings one was taught to have." Again, in the same way as with awareness, the mentally retarded have been spared from *learning* the feelings they *ought* to have. It has been observed how the men are very free with regards to their feelings. They have little hesitancy in showing both their affection or their disaffection, either by gesture or word. One day, for example, Madame Vanier, who in the beginning spent a month at Trosly each summer and has now settled there permanently, invited Michel to come to her home for lunch. She asked him if he would like someone else to join them. "Yes," he said, "Zizi." Madame Vanier discovered, however, that Zizi was not free that day. She went and informed Michel that his friend would not be there for lunch. "Well, I'm not coming then," he said; "I don't want to eat with you alone."

Finally, intimacy is defined as the "spontaneous, game-free candidness of an aware person, the liberation of the essentially perceptive, uncorrupted Child in all its naiveté living in the here and now." Candidness is also a quality attributed to the men at l'Arche. This candidness, Berne notes, is what can evoke affection in others. Those who have lived at l'Arche have, in fact been drawn into intimacy with the men because of this candidness. Barbara Z, a kind of American gypsy who has lived in many parts of the world, wandered into Trosly and stayed for many months. She tells the story of the deep intimacy that she experienced there with many, but especially with Ange. One day she was afflicted with diarrhea. She was rushing through the house with the desperate and single-minded intention of getting to the toilet before it was too late. Ange heard her come in and, as she passed his room, in his gentle way he called her name, "Barbara!" She says that to her own amazement she stopped at once and went to Ange. How the episode ended she did not say. All this helps us to understand the importance of childlikeness that is so much stressed in the Gospels (Unless you become as little children you cannot enter the Kingdom), as well as helping us to understand the deep faith that has been attributed to the men of l'Arche. Childlikeness makes possible an intimate relation with others, as well as with the Other. As Berne says, "Before, unless and until they are corrupted, most infants seem to be loving, and that is the essential nature of intimacy." To a greater degree than most people, the mentally retarded seem to maintain uncorrupted this capacity for love. People who go there are usually touched by the capacity of these people to love on the human level, as well as their deep, unquestioning faith, and especially their intimacy with the person of Jesus. As Francoise, a truly radiant young French woman, says:

> It is there that I learned to love and where I received so much. It is not something you learn – it is something you receive. It is not ourselves in any way at all who achieve this. It is He who teaches us – like that – to receive – and our hands like that (open) – that's all.

These qualities of the people he had felt called to help were making their impact on Vanier directly as well as from the way he was seeing them change others who had come to work with him. In proportion to the limitations in the power of reasoning, it seems that people are enriched in the gifts of the heart. These gifts of the heart are precisely what are so greatly needed in a technological society that is becoming ever more heartless. Vanier's vision was shifting from a concern for what society could do for the handicapped to a concern for what the handicapped could do for society.

Throughout these early years the community of l'Arche was growing. Other houses in Trosly were purchased to begin new homes. As l'Arche grew and became better known there was a lengthening waiting list of men and women who could no longer be cared for by parents or find adequate accommodations in institutions. Furthermore, it was becoming increasingly evident how unjust it is that such people should be confined in psychiatric hospitals which are really little more than prisons. Vanier realized, as he says, that:

> Our center must not be a ghetto where a few handicapped can live happily. We must constantly strive to bring a realistic solution to a human and social problem, that of the handicapped in our modern society. We would like to see l'Arche become a prototype or model for the creation of other centers and for those who are working for justice in this area.

So the seeds of new communities started to take root beyond the village of Trosly. Valinos, a center for women, was begun in the nearby town of Cuise-la-Motte. La Merci, a center for men and women, was begun further south in the Cognac region of France. Then a similar center called Daybreak was begun in Canada, just north of Toronto. Asha Niketan was then opened in Bangalore, India. Finally, in the past year (1972-1973), l'Arche communities have been inaugurated in Ottawa, Cornwall, Stratford, Edmonton, Winnipeg, Erie (Pennsylvania), Canterbury (England), Copenhagen, Calcutta, and several areas of France.

The opening of communities in India has been especially significant. This has given Vanier a direct contact with the Third World. He has found that it has been very meaningful for the men and women at l'Arche to have their own vision opened to the entire world. In this regard he says:

> The opening out of the spirit of the handicapped through their awareness of foundations on other continents will be enormously beneficial to them on the human, cultural and spiritual plane. Does not the dignity of man come precisely from this opening out towards the universal?

It calls forth in a special way their great capacity for compassion. The prayerful concern that they express for Asha Niketan and all the poor of India is very genuine and moving. At various times of the year one of the men at l'Arche, Jacques, takes it upon himself to collect money and send it to Gabrielle for her work in India. This contact with the Third World has deepened Vanier's sensitivity to the widening gap between the rich and poor of the world. He sees his communities as a contribution towards bridging this gap.

The faith dimension of this work was evident from the beginning, but this was gradually being deepened. It was especially the openness to the faith on the part of the more simple members of the community, cultivated as it was by the attentive ministry of Père Thomas that was effecting this deepening. Also, it seemed that only by the spirit of the Gospel could one continue in this way of life. Vanier underlines this fact:

> I have come to realize with ever greater clarity that to live with the handicapped we must be penetrated with the values of the Gospel (respect for the human person, especially the most fragile; the primacy of compassion over efficiency and productivity). . . . Our community implies two aspects: an element of faith which is central, and a more human element of psychological progress, culture, work, and so forth. It is realized in the profound love which unites us and makes us happy to live together in mutual respect without necessarily practicing the same faith, and in the joy of seeing one another progress in the ways of the Holy Spirit.

This movement was manifested in Vanier's lectures which were becoming more spiritual in their orientation, more explicitly inspired by the message of the Gospel.

In 1968 some Catholic priests in Toronto invited him to preach a retreat to them. He accepted on the condition that it be not just for priests but for sisters and lay people, young and old, and people suffering from various physical or mental handicaps. He also asked that there be the chance for these people to share together in ways that would allow them to enrich one another. The sixty people who made this week-long experience of "Faith and Sharing" were profoundly touched by it. Thus began a new dimension of Vanier's life. He was beginning to share with many others the Gospel message of liberation and hope that he was assimilating in his life at l'Arche. Since that time he has been taking this message to a widening circle of leaders in society, but especially to the wounded and rejected people themselves. This past year he has met and spoken to inmates in almost all the major prisons and psychiatric hospitals in Canada. At the request of the prisoners themselves he spent two days in Drumheller prison, living in a cell and sharing with the men. Recently he directed a five-day National Ecumenical Retreat. This brought together about a hundred English and French speaking people from across Canada. There was a cross-section of clergy and lay people from the major Christian denominations, including the Moderator of the United Church, and Bishops of the Anglican and Roman Catholic Churches. To these people he is trying to reveal what he has been discovering in his own community: that each person, no matter how wounded he may be, has a great dignity and the capacity to enrich others. He speaks of his own growing awareness of the fact that Jesus' saving work was finally accomplished through his dying among common criminals, as an outcast of society. The passages of scripture which have special meaning for him are: "The very stone which the builders rejected has become the chief cornerstone; this was the Lord's doing, and it is marvelous to see!" (Mk. 11:10) and "The weak things of this earth God has chosen to confound the wise." (1 Cor. 1:27)

The communities of l'Arche are a proclamation that salvation comes through the little people, the wounded and rejected of the world.

Healing presences:
around Lucien's stamp collection (*top*); through Jean-Michel's sense of touch.

CHAPTER FOUR

Keeping It Afloat

"This is a magnificent ideal, but it is impossible to live." This was the conclusion of a journalist from a well-known French magazine after she had spent a morning at Trosly visiting the homes and workshops and talking with Jean Vanier about his vision of l'Arche. Vanier himself speaks of it as a kind of foolishness: "This folly is the very basis of our community: to accept to live with the handicapped and in a certain way to identify with them, without renouncing our responsibilities." Is it liveable or not? We want now to examine the actual structure and organization, particularly that of the community at Trosly, to see how this vision has taken on flesh and bones and become a living reality.

If in the beginning l'Arche was simply a small charismatic retinue, a group of friends led and inspired by Jean Vanier, there was nonetheless some sharing of the responsibility and authority. Vanier had some idea about what l'Arche might be, but he was also searching and eager to learn from the men and the assistants. It was already noted in discussing the aims that the first few months of living with the men did much to change and broaden his idea of l'Arche. It would seem, and this naturally enough, that the first assistants to join Vanier did not immediately grasp and share his vision. But gradually, as more and more come to share in this vision there is a growing sense that they are all joined together in a common adventure, in a new way of working with the mentally handicapped, in a new type of Christian community without precedent or prototype. So too, with Vanier himself, the sense of adventure and the element of search has only become more acute with each new element that is introduced, be it the opening of a house in India, or the creation of an experimental workshop at Trosly.

There has been, however, a gradual shift in the organization, from a charismatic retinue to a more professional type of organization (although Vanier's inspirational leadership is every bit as important today as it was in the beginning). Such a shift implies an ever greater sharing of everything from the vision and theory, to the deployment of resources, the division of responsibility, the supervision and discipline. One very important characteristic of this shift is that it has been a question of organic growth. A structure has not been conceived in an *a priori* manner and imposed from above, but has rather been something growing out of the concrete exigencies of the work and life of the community. The structure has remained in the service of, and not prior to personal relations.

This organic growth of the structure has itself been structured into l'Arche, in the form of a yearly meeting in which the entire structure is put into question and renovated in terms of present needs and future expectations. This meeting is a weekend of discussions, reflection, prayer and decision-making which reviews the past year and plans for the coming year. This yearly meeting that insures a dynamically evolving structure has itself evolved with the increasing dimensions of the community. For example, last year was the first time that it was split into two parts, one weekend given to studying the more temporal aspects of l'Arche, and another given to a more prayerful reflection on the spiritual needs of the community.

After some discussion it was decided not to have the men and women participate in the meeting dealing with the questions of organization, work, pedagogy and so forth. Few of them would have been concerned with, or able to grasp the significance of most of these issues. Also some of the assistants felt it would be hard to talk freely of pedagogical issues in the presence of the men and women. This meeting, then, was only for the assistants. All of them, even the most recent arrivals were invited to participate in the discussion (a list of 60 persons in all). The right to vote was restricted to those who had been at l'Arche for at least six months (54 persons).

So this yearly meeting gives all the assistants, even those most recently arrived, the opportunity to participate in shaping the organization of the life and work of l'Arche. Such a structure helps to very quickly integrate new members into the community, giving them a real share in the responsibility at a very basic level. It also helps the new arrivals to understand by a rather direct experience how in fact the community is structured. What they cannot help but sense here as well as in the day-to-day living at l'Arche is its provisional aspect. Its organization is not defined by a written constitution as, for example, is done in most religious communities so that basic elements of their structure are established in a rather definitive way. The organization of l'Arche is set up only a year at a time, thus giving it a great deal of flexibility. This flexibility and provisional nature reflect the aspect of adventure and search which is an important element of its spirit. With the opportunity to share very quickly in the responsibility for the growth and direction of the community, the assistants are soon caught up into a sense of a common adventure.

Jean Vanier has felt it of great importance to try and maintain this twofold element of the provisional and flexible as l'Arche has grown and its structure become more complex. Any organization as it grows larger naturally tends to become more structured and institutionalized. L'Arche has not been totally exempt from this tendency. If we look at its present form of government, for example, we shall see that it has become an institution with little resemblance to the original gathering of a few friends around the person of Vanier.

The government of l'Arche was one of the major areas of discussion during last year's meeting, and it underwent considerable changes, as it has almost every year. This year the post of sub-director was created, to help supply for Vanier's increasing absences, and to help shoulder the increasing administrative burdens. Certainly, part of the reason for creating this post was also the presence of Miss Maurice, who was the obvious person to fill it. Other changes were effected so that now it consists of a director, sub-director, a major council, a council of those in positions of responsibility, and a general assembly. The major council consists of the director and sub-director, three elected members, and two members named by the director (one of whom happens to be Père Thomas). This council has the power to make major decisions, nominate to major positions or change those in major positions, accept or dismiss assistants, open new homes, and so forth. The second council is consultative and informative for the concerns of the major council and decision-making for all current affairs. It includes the director, the heads of the various homes, the director and assistant director of the workshops, the nurse, social worker, psychologist, secretary, and several other people responsible in different areas. The members of this council represent all the members of the community, and can make decisions concerning the normal function of the community. Each of these councils meets once a week, and when specially convoked to deal with a specific problem. The general assembly is made up of all the assistants. It meets every Monday morning to plan for the coming week, and make certain more long-range plans.

This form of government is ordered towards giving a very high degree of participation on all levels at which responsibility is exercised. The annual report recently drawn up by Vanier notes, however, one evident lack in this participation which he hopes to see remedied in the coming years: namely, that of having some of the handicapped themselves elected to participate at some of these levels of responsibility. An obvious disadvantage in having such wide participation is that much time is given to meetings, thus taking the assistants away from their particular responsibilities, and leaving them that much less time to be present to the men and women. This, however, is not a serious difficulty. The problem at l'Arche that is presently rather critical is not the communion between the assistants and the handicapped, but rather among the assistants themselves. Ways have been considered for trying to supply for a certain lack of communion among the assistants that many of them feel and sometimes complain about. The widespread participation in responsibility also gives rise to a certain over-lapping and confusion of responsibility. As one man describes it:

> In a community like that, because everyone lives so closely together it's hard to know what position each person has, especially from the administrative point of view. I was often ordering supplies for work and it was interesting knowing who I was supposed to go to, or who I was to talk to to borrow stepladders and that sort of thing. There's Mr. Vanier at the top and then there's three or four people under him, each one has a different duty but it isn't precisely defined. Then down below that you have people in the *foyers*, and – well, I wouldn't want to say too much about it, but many times we did have difficulties as far as who really has the responsibility, perhaps better put, who can really accept the responsibility and be head of the *foyer*, and how do the duties work out. If one person has the responsibility of the *foyer* what duties are expected of him. I think this is sort of what bothered me most because you weren't quite sure of your own position and what you were supposed to be doing when it wasn't clear from the top down. Well, you wouldn't want it to be too professional, too clearcut. It's not a matter of one person giving orders to another person. You work together, but it does get confusing at times. I don't know whether this is Trosly or the French way of doing things but

I'd say things do get into a mess. It gets to be a joke after a while. It all works out in the end.

This difficulty is mitigated by the climate of friendship and respectful personal contact in which are carried out the various exchanges of authority and responsibility. The frustration that is sometimes born of this confusion more often culminates in laughter or the exclamation "Alleluia," than in an expression of anger. There is also a certain structure, the general assembly, that allows for dialogue between the various levels of responsibility and so the possibility of working out some of these communication problems.

The general assembly which meets weekly for about an hour and a half manifests both the element of widespread participation and the personal character of the government. This meeting is chaired by Jean Vanier, or in his absence by the sub-directress, Miss Maurice. All the assistants who can make it to this meeting are gathered more or less in a circle but quite informally with no privileged positions. Vanier has the habit of showing a special warmth to those who have the humblest tasks in the community and who perhaps tend to be the most withdrawn. For example, when someone like the little, elderly lady who helps with the house-keeping arrives, he welcomes her with a big smile and invites her to sit next to him. In the discussions that ensue he is careful to elicit the opinions of those who tend to be more quiet and shy. The whole tenor of this meeting is one of relaxed friendship, where there is much laughter and only very rarely any tension and heated discussion. Here there is an opportunity to freely express one's opinion or difficulties in the various aspects of the community's functioning. Fernand, who is in charge of the sports program, might raise the issue of preparations for the forthcoming special olympics for the mentally retarded. Anne-Marie, the psychologist, might speak of a man who is just finishing his first two-weeks trial period at l'Arche, asking if this trial has indicated that l'Arche is good for him, and whether or not he should be brought back for a second trial of one or two months. Planning for a picnic or a day of spiritual renewel can be discussed with regards to the various aspects: Michel giving his opinion insofar as it may involve closing the workshops early, others giving their opinion with regard to the transportation, or the preparing of meals or the coordination between the various homes, and so forth. So there is dialogue established between people in various areas of responsibility; between the more permanent assistants and the newly arrived, between those who live in the homes and those who come daily to work in the infirmary or the workshops or laundry and the like, between those more concerned with the religious aspects of the community and those more concerned with the material aspects. This general assembly contributes to the provisional and flexible aspects of l'Arche. Besides the long-range planning, there is this weekly planning and flexible adjustment to whatever unsuspected needs might arise from within or from the exterior. Decisions made by the council can in this general assembly be communicated directly to all the assistants, and through them to the entire community.

The provisional and flexible aspects also imply a certain fragility and vulnerability. It means not only that the community can evolve but also that it can disintegrate. There is here a rather remarkable contrast with such professional organizations as hospitals or such communities as the more traditional religious orders. Both of these types of organizations are very highly structured in a way that protects them against adverse change, or any change whatever, for that matter. To consider only the aspect of the assimilation of new members, the difference is seen to be striking. In a hospital, for example, not only do nurses have no say in the organization during their years of formation, but even as graduates they have little or no responsibility in shaping the organization. This, of course, is even more true for the orderlies, the maintenance staff and so forth, not to mention the patients themselves who are fairly well reduced to passive objects. In contrast, the community at l'Arche is vulnerable to being changed by people who have had little time to be imbued with its spirit and meaning. This vulnerability is very real since, in fact, about half of those who had a vote in the last yearly meeting had been at l'Arche less than two years.

This vulnerability or fragility, however, has a few obvious advantages. We have already mentioned the matter of integrating new members more quickly and totally into the community. Along with this comes the influx of new ideas and new life that these people bring to the community. The natural tendency of older members to become somewhat staid or self-satisfied is counter-acted by the active participation of new members who are continually arriving. The that's-the-way-we've-always-done-things attitude is constantly being challenged by those who do not know and perhaps do not particularly care how things have *always* been done. In the same way the newly arrived mentally handicapped also, because of the great freedom that is given to them, continue to challenge and put in question the "traditional" or "normal" ways of doing things.

An extremely important advantage of this fragile structure is the way it makes the entire community more responsive to the individual needs of the handicapped. Dr. Richet, who was the psychiatrist that assisted l'Arche in its early days and who remains very close to it, mentioned this fragility as one of l'Arche's most powerful means of helping the handicapped. She contrasts it to the mental hospital where many of the men and women of l'Arche have come. The hospital in its physical plant, its financial and governmental structure is solid and unshakeable. This very solidity makes it terribly unresponsive and insensitive to the needs of its inmates. L'Arche, on the other hand, she notes, is an extremely fragile sort of thing: a group of typical, modest houses spread out in the village, with limited financial resources, with only a bare minimum of professionally trained staff, greatly dependent on volunteer help, capable of falling apart at any moment. But this very fragility makes it so much more sensitive to the individual members and flexible enough to respond to the unique needs of each.

Finally, this fragility calls for greater dependence on Divine Providence and a greater openness to the Spirit. Many speak of "a spiritual force" keeping the community going, and of the spirit of trust in Divine Providence. Others add that their own trust in Providence had been greatly increased as a result of being there. Some of this was attributed to Jean Vanier's own faith, and to certain values predominant in the mentally handicapped, but also to "the lack of a strong organizational structure," "the lack of material wealth," and "the openness to anyone who comes along," in other words, to this element of fragility. The more an individual or a community can rely on their own strength, on their human capacities and material resources the less they experience their need to rely on others. We saw that the very fragility of the handicapped disposed them in a unique way to depend on others and on the Other. So this quality or personality structure of feeling the need for help that is peculiar to the handicapped is reflected on the level of the structure and organization of the community as a whole.

Coupled with this aspect of fragility is that of the provisional and evolving. The community is on the move, but no one is sure where it is going. There is no prototype and few guidelines, so there is a deeply felt need to get guidance from somewhere. This experience of needing guidance disposes the community towards a real openness to the Spirit. This aspect of the community's structure perhaps is more a reflection of a certain disposition of many of the assistants, rather than of the men and womễn. It is the assistants who more consciously bear the responsibility for the growth and direction of the community. Also it is the assistants who are more consciously concerned about the direction of their own lives. Many have given themselves quite totally to l'Arche. On the other hand, many of the assistants at l'Arche who at least in their own hearts have made some sort of commitment to the community remain in great uncertainty. Not only do they live in the incertitude that their own commitment is not definitively determined, but also that of knowing that it is the same case for all the others with whom and to whom they are committed. Furthermore, they live with the awareness that neither they or anyone else quite knows where the community is going. So there is a kind of risk and uncertainty that can be very painful but which greatly disposes them to a constant recourse to the Spirit for guidance.

The various degrees of commitment and levels of participation of l'Arche's members also make of it what can best be described as an open community.

First, with regard to duration. We have noted that there are many people who come to l'Arche only for a limited time. This limit may or may not be fixed in advance. Patrick came for "two days," and left seven months later. John was picked up by a carload of l'Arche people who were returning to Trosly after a weekend at Ambleteuse. He was hitch-hiking from England to Spain at the time. With little fixed destination and deadlines there was no reason not to stop in at Trosly. Four months later he is still there with no plans to move on. Only rarely does it work the other way: where someone plans to stay maybe a year but then leaves before this period has been completed. In any case, there is a constant flow of people. They come for a few weeks, a few months, a year or more. They share in the life and work of the community, giving of themselves, of their time and talents, receiving much in return and then finally moving on. Bonds of friendship are created that make departures very difficult, but there is rarely any sense of defeat or failure, and these bonds remain intact. The primary task of l'Arche is to help those who live there, first the handicapped and secondly the assistants, to achieve the greatest possible human and spiritual progress. This task is in no way frustrated by such a continual flow of people coming and going. It is quite the contrary, because such a primary task is founded on an openness and mutual respect by which each can achieve the maximum liberty that is possible to him.

With regard to the degree of commitment there is also great flexibility. At l'Arche it is not an all-or-nothing proposition. Some commit themselves only with regard to their professional services, coming perhaps from some distance to spend their eight hours a day at l'Arche and then returning to their home and family or to their bachelor apartment or wherever they may live. It is possible that they be a member of a religious congregation. Presently, there is one nun who comes to Trosly to run one of the workshops. She returns each evening to her little community of sisters in another village several miles away. It is with that community that she shares her domestic life, leisure time and life of worship. Even for these people l'Arche is not just another place to work. Their work there has also a certain element of gratuity and self-gift. They may or may not share quite considerably in the life of faith and worship but because the life calls forth this gift of self they are very much a part of the community.

On the other hand, there are a few people who have their life and work quite apart from l'Arche, but who share to a great extent in the faith-life and worship of the community. There is, for example, the growing number of French college students who often come to Trosly for the weekends or for a week or two at a time. Several of them have been converted or re-converted to the faith under the influence and direction of Père Thomas. To facilitate their coming and going, several years ago there was a little home, La Grange, that Père Thomas placed at their disposal. La Grange is off to one corner of the village and is independent of the l'Arche administration. More recently la Ferme, a complex of lodgings, library and chapel clustered around a courtyard, has been established to this same end. Besides the handful of local villagers who participate at least in the Sunday worship and other personal ministries of Père Thomas, there are one or two people who have come to live permanently at Trosly precisely to be able to share in the faith-life and worship while otherwise living quite independently of l'Arche. Other friends of l'Arche are planning to do likewise.

There are many others committed to l'Arche on a more full time basis, with that sort of total gift that is characteristic of religious consecration. These are especially the people who live in the homes with the men and women. But even here there is a multiplicity of variations. Most of them are presently unmarried. Some have the intention of remaining so as the style by which they feel called to love and serve the Lord in and through this community. A couple are widows. There are also a few married couples with or without families. There are also consecrated religious, such as Père Thomas himself who it seems will remain at Trosly for the rest of his days but continues a limited contact with his confrères and obedience to his superiors in the Dominican Order. And there are a few religious, especially North American Jesuits, who participate totally in the l'Arche community for three or four months during the summer or even for a year or more at a time.

It should be noted that Père Thomas who is so much at the heart of the community actually lives quite apart from the other members. His home is one small room behind the sacristy. There he lives quite poorly: praying, preparing his sermons and talks, counselling a number of the men and women and assistants and others who come to see him. He does a considerable amount of visiting the sick and those in the nearby mental hospital, participates in council meetings, but only rarely accepts invitations to take a meal or participate in other social events in the homes. But this withdrawal is not to make him less present to the community. Quite the contrary, he is most present, being totally given to the community, in a very clear and unambiguous way, as a man of the Spirit.

A few others also live this more secluded type of existence at the heart of the community. These are people who participate quite fully in the work, direction, faith and worship of the community but who have their little home or couple of rooms apart in the village, where they have the possibility of greater silence. These also are not less present to the community, but simply live a more contemplative life within it.

Finally, there are also a few assistants who participate in almost everything except the faith life and worship. I personally know several people who live or have lived at l'Arche while not participating in the faith life and worship. Most of them admit to sometimes feeling a bit left out of things, but they are grateful for the freedom that is given to live there on these conditions.

A further variation to this already wide variety of levels of participation is the matter of financial remuneration. Here the range is from those who are paid a full salary from the moment of their arrival to those who are full time at l'Arche while refusing any salary whatsoever. The normal procedure, although there are some exceptions to this, is that those who come with professional skills are paid the current salary for such skills. Those who come without such skills and more as volunteers who wish to share in an experience of community receive no money except a small amount of spending money if they commit themselves to stay for about a year. If at the end of a year they wish to commit themselves on a more permanent basis and their presence and work is judged by the major council as adequate, they will be offered a regular salary. A few actually return a part or all of this salary out of a desire to live in a greater spirit of evangelical poverty.

It is important to note that the amount of salary received is little indication, one way or another, of the degree of generosity and self-gift by which the individual might be committed to l'Arche. There are some who receive quite a good salary, and who live elsewhere than at Trosly, yet whose dedication to the men and women and to the whole work of l'Arche is most outstanding. Others who might be at Trosly on a volunteer basis, receiving no salary, sometimes manifest less of this quality of self-gift and presence. Furthermore, it is not always those who participate most fully in the life of worship who manifest the greatest generosity in giving of themselves.

There can be discerned a certain central core or inner circle of assistants who assure an element of stability for the life and spirit of the community. This is a group of about fifteen people, or a few more or less depending on the radius one might choose to draw the circle around Jean Vanier, or perhaps, better, draw the elipse around Jean Vanier and Père Thomas. This is not a juridicial entity, although it includes all those in the major council and many of those in the secondary council. A couple of years ago there was an effort made to give a juridical structure to just such a central core by creating a group of "permanent assistants" personally committed to uphold the spirit defined by the statutes. They had the power to decide for or against accepting assistants on a permanent basis after their first year at l'Arche. They also were empowered to elect a new director after the retirement or death of Jean Vanier. For various reasons this organization of "permanent assistants" never really proved satisfactory. For one thing, the statutes are presently of little significance. Furthermore, the last restructuring of the organization took away the only authority that the "permanent assistants" had, by giving to the major council the authority to accept or dismiss assistants, and giving voting

61

rights to all who have been at l'Arche for at least six months. It remains to be seen whether or not some new definition will be given to the "permanent assistants." In any case, for the present, the real central core of assistants is a group without juridical definition. Most of these participate rather fully in the faith-life and worship of the community, but there are one or two exceptions. In fact, it comprises almost the whole gamut of variations of levels of participation that have just been outlined.

It is important to note here that it is not only the assistants, or a core group of assistants who assure a certain stability and spirit in the community. The handicapped themselves are very much responsible for the spirit of the community, and are finally the real guarantees of its stability. There is, in fact, a far greater turnover of assistants than of the men and women. There are at least a dozen men who have been at Trosly since the founding of the Val Fleuri some ten years ago; that is to say, they have been there even longer than Jean Vanier himself. Three of the original four men that he took in during the first months to initiate his little home of l'Arche are still there. The men and women maintain the spirit of the community with little conscious effort, by their natural simplicity, openness and capacity for affection. It would perhaps be more accurate to say that the assistants are there to animate these people and call forth their gifts. They have the responsibility to ensure that, with the growth and evolution that is taking place, the organization and structure of the community remains at the service of the person.

There is also among the men and women considerable variety with regard to their level of participation in and commitment to the community. Besides the large number who live at Trosly there are also a sizeable group who live in family placements or foster homes, and a group who live at home with parents or other relatives. The latter two groups come to work at l'Arche and form something of a basic community among themselves and the assistants with whom they share the noon meal. A few of the men and women who live in have their work outside in factories, shops or elsewhere quite independently from l'Arche. Some of them have a very strong sense that their stay at l'Arche is only a stage towards integration into "normal" society. A few have a sense that l'Arche is where they will live out the rest of their lives. Some are very uncertain about this issue, and a few are perhaps not aware enough to consider the question. Some are quite capable of organizing most of their own leisure, while others depend very much on the assistants in this regard. Some participate quite fully in the faith-life and worship, others only minimally and some not at all. Some have very good relations with their families and spend every weekend and holiday with them, while others see their families rarely or not at all. For a few of the men and women l'Arche is just another institution to which they have been committed, perhaps somewhat better than the last one they were in, but still an institution. A fair number do have a sense of the mission of l'Arche as a Christian community witnessing to the Gospel by its spirit of unity, peace and joy. A small but growing number at least consider the possibility of a personal call to commit themselves to live out their faith in Jesus in and through l'Arche.

L'Arche is also an open community in that the external boundary is such as to allow for participation at many different levels or degrees. For one thing, this means that some members of the community will find their primary support relationships elsewhere, either in their families, their religious congregations, or with other friends, thus keeping the community inserted into the greater society in a vital way. It cannot easily become a ghetto or a sect. Such openness also allows for a good deal of personal freedom. There is no forcing the individual to commit himself to more than he is ready for, or to assume certain responsibilities simply out of the necessity of taking a "package deal", as in the Roman rite of the Catholic Church where one has no choice but to be celibate if he wishes to be a priest (a practice that has its own merits).

The freedom to participate in the faith-life and worship as one feels the need or the call encourages a personal and interior appropriation of the faith. No doubt some people would profit more from a situation that was more structured and that imposed certain religious practices by rule, but at least here there is a high degree of authenticity. People pray and worship not because of any exterior law but because of some inner need or call.

Furthermore, with its wide variety of participants l'Arche in some ways embodies all the different elements of the whole Church. It is an instance of the universal Christian community. L'Arche is a community of: laymen, religious and priests; married people, single people and widows; those who have freely chosen to be celibate and those condemned to it by nature or circumstances; believers, catechumens and those still in search; some whose vocation is more contemplative, and others more active, and some whose vocation is more charismatic; Catholics and Protestants, traditionalists and progressives, old and young, rich and poor. This vast variety are all together working for a common goal in a common spirit. With such a variety of people meeting one another precisely as people in all their uniqueness there is necessarily generated a tremendous amount of creativity and life.

To this point, all that has been said about the organization and structure has been mainly with regard to the community at Trosly. It remains to say something about l'Arche taken in the widest sense to include the other communities in France and elsewhere.

The bonds between these various communities are primarily spiritual bonds, that is, of friendship, and of the inspiration of Jean Vanier, and the concern to live out a common vision. All the communities of France have the same overall board of directors, with Jean Vanier as the president. However, the director of each of the communities is given a great deal of freedom to run his community as he or she thinks best. An example of this freedom is the case of one of the communities where the directress took quite an independent attitude to Trosly. Her approach was to treat the handicapped as patients to be cured, rather than simply as people with whom to share life. She was given the freedom to pursue this approach, but it proved quite unsuccessful, and the board of directors had to move in in order to save the situation. This experience pointed out the risk of giving so much liberty to the different directors, but it did not provoke any change in this policy.

The board of directors is the organization with ultimate responsibility for all the l'Arche communities in France. It is recognized by the government and receives through social security and social welfare the necessary funds for the daily running of these communities. Each centre presents a yearly budget to be approved by the prefecture of the department of France in which it is located. This budget is worked out on the basis of the daily cost per mentally handicapped in the centre. The parents of the handicapped who can afford it refund to the government whatever portion of this cost that they can comfortably assume. This system assures the daily running expenses but it also imposes on the community the obligation of a careful control of its spending. For expansion and the improvement of facilities or unexpected expenditures, money must be acquired elsewhere, from private donations, loans and so forth. At the present time enough money is forthcoming to allow a fairly rapid expansion. Whatever money comes in, is quickly spent to purchase more property or make other improvements to accommodate the mounting population of mentally handicapped, who have no work and who often live in very inhuman conditions.

This financial structure may not impose on the members of l'Arche a life that can be called poor, but it does imply a very modest kind of living. At least there is nothing fictitious about the spirit of poverty of those who must constantly struggle to keep the food costs and other spending reasonably within the *per diem* cost allowed for by the budget. More importantly, this structure is a guarantee that the community not become a sect or closed little world, with minimal reference to the larger society. Whatever may be the spiritual aspirations or religious ambience of the community it must remain relevant to the larger community in which it is firmly rooted and to which it is always answerable.

Until 1972 the communities outside of France were totally independent structurally from one another and from Trosly. Then in 1972 the directors of all these communities met in Trosly and formed the Federation of l'Arche, a very loose bond that leaves each member community free to develop according to its needs, allowing it to be more integral to its own society and culture.

Jean Vanier in person is actually the strongest link between all these communities. He was on hand in Bangalore when Asha Niketan (Homes of Hope) opened its doors to its first handicapped men. He remained there with them for a month. Now every year he spends one month in India. On his last trip the groundwork was laid for the new Asha Niketan in Calcutta. On his twice-yearly trips to North America he manages to spend some time at Daybreak, Alleluia House, Mary Farm, the Hearth and the other members of the Federation. His role in these communities is not that of a superior or director but as a friend, advisor and inspirational guide.

The unity of spirit is also due to the fact that, as it happens, in all the centres the director and/or some of the assistants have lived and worked for some time in the community of Trosly. This has created very deep bonds of friendship between the assistants and also between assistants and the handicapped in different centres. The joy with which Agnes and Adriano from La Merci, for example, are welcomed at Trosly is an obvious indication of this deep friendship. The various communities in France also have frequent exchange visits of

65

small groups or even of the entire community, so that friendships between the handicapped in different centres are also developing.

Since each of the centres has considerable independence, each has taken on quite a unique character, although there is a certain spirit that is common to them all – the same spirit that animates Trosly. There is at least one unique characteristic that distinguishes each of the subsequent foundations from the mother community of Trosly. Valinos is a centre for women, begun with a woman at its head. La Merci began not as a home but simply a protected workshop, for men and women, under the direction of a married couple but with the wife actually in charge. (The husband is finishing a doctorate in philosophy.) The Tremplin (more closely united to Trosly) is a half-way house for men and women moving towards integration into society. One of these men is soon to be married. All of its handicapped work in factories and shops in the city. It is run by a retired industrialist. Daybreak is also run by a married couple, with the husband actually in charge. This is the first centre to have a director that is not Roman Catholic. Steven and Ann are Anglicans. The property was the gift of a congregation of Sisters (Our Lady's Missionaries). These Sisters and many other friends are Catholic, so the community has a very decidedly ecumenical spirit. Asha Niketan is the first centre to be founded in the Third World. Although Gabrielle, the directress, is not Indian, she is making every effort to make her community an integral part of the society and culture of Bangalore. The board of directors is all Indian, and the spirit is ecumenical, with Catholics and Hindus praying together daily.

The exchanges between these communities is particularly enriching precisely because of this plurality of characteristics. As the mother community continues to expand and evolve, it draws on the experience of these other centres, constantly appropriating and assimilating what it is receiving from them, and in turn nourishing them with something of its own life and character.

The very fragility of the bonds that link these various communities calls forth a need and desire for an ever deeper spiritual unity. One senses this very much, for example, at Trosly in the intensity with which they pray for the other communities (often mentioning by name the directors and other members) at the Eucharist and other prayer meetings and in the evening prayer in the individual homes. The Faith and Light International Pilgrimage for the Mentally Handicapped that took place at Lourdes on Easter 1971 was a rare opportunity for the various communities of l'Arche to come together, and thus strengthen this unity. The whole or most of the members of each community, assistants and handicapped, were present, some two hundred people in all. Asha Niketan was the only community not represented. Their absence was felt rather deeply, and they were in some way made present in the spirit by the way they were thought of and prayed for by those who were there. Besides meeting frequently during the pilgrimage itself the communities spent a day together after the pilgrimage officially ended.

The whole tone of this encounter perhaps symbolizes something of what l'Arche is all about. There were no big discussions on policy or structure and organization. From the late afternoon when they gathered until the next morning when they separated, the whole atmosphere was one of joyful celebration. They played, sang, danced and prayed together in a joyful spirit of friendship and unity. Young men and women (and some not so young) from Canada met and were immediately at one with those of the different centres of France. The fact that the latter spoke only French posed little or no barriers to the communication. They all spoke a common language, the language of the Child which most of us have long forgotten. As the various groups parted to return to their own centres, the singing and dancing, the embraces and handshakes, the laughter and the tears clearly showed that the real force that guaranteed a continuing communion was the power of the Spirit at work in their hearts.

This "power of the Spirit" is finally the only explanation for the continuing survival and growth of l'Arche. However much has been said about its organization and structure, the structure in fact is much less visible than it may appear from this chapter. People who have been there know that something beyond the structure is keeping it all going. As one person remarks:

> It had already been going about five years when I went there. I was there about a month or a month and a half before I realized that there is a spiritual force that must be keeping it together because it is so loosely organized.

Another speaks of it in a similar way:

> Sometimes you feel that the way the place is run, the way they are open to everybody and the amount of stuff that they put up with – this is absolute folly what they are trying to do. Then you stand back after three months and you look and you say, "It works, for some reason or other." Also,

there are a lot of tensions there and the whole show could just go up in smoke tomorrow, yet somehow or other it doesn't. It just keeps on going and fantastic things happen. It's just this unbelievable trust that impressed me – a trust that God will work this thing out.

Certainly some of the success is due to the genius and charism of Jean Vanier, as someone pointed out: "Vanier has the genius of keeping this unstructured thing going, and it works." Another noted:

It's like today. All week long we had been planning to go to the sea today, and all week long it has rained. So today it's nice out. Everybody says it's a kind of *Vanierism* – you just hope for the best and it always works out.

However, it is obviously something more than Jean Vanier that is keeping l'Arche going. Everyone who lives there is convinced of this. One man puts it quite simply, and speaks for many there when he says: "It is something deeper than the influence of Mr. Vanier – I think it is the presence of Christ." It is certainly this belief that holds many at l'Arche and so makes it a living organism.

Jean Vanier: encouraging (*top*);
listening — the Monday morning meeting.

Giving thanks: the Eucharist (*top*);
before dinner at La Source.

CHAPTER FIVE

The Pain of It All

Almost everyone who comes to l'Arche is immediately impressed by the spirit of joy that prevails there. Yet anyone who comes to know the community more intimately cannot but be impressed, not to say overwhelmed, by the amount of suffering that is simply a part of its daily life. The living out in great intensity of these seemingly opposite experiences, joy and suffering, might be called the particular grace or vocation of l'Arche. Both the suffering and the joy are an integral part of the daily existence, but both have their moments of greater intensity and more external expression. There are the instances of crises and there is death that crystalize the suffering. The joy reaches its climax in moments of celebration. The one, however, is never entirely without the other, especially because both find their ultimate meaning in the single mystery – birth, death, and resurrection – the total mystery of life.

Perhaps almost enough has been said already concerning the suffering of the handicapped which is essentially that of rejection, of being categorized as different and inferior. For those who would protest that such people are not conscious enough to recognize the looks of disdain, pity or fear that are constantly being cast at them, we need only remind them that even a little baby whose intellect has scarcely begun to function knows instinctively if he is loved or not. Furthermore, his continuing growth, even his very survival, depend on his receiving not only physical protection and nourishment but also of receiving a certain amount of acceptance and human affection. It is true that having lived this experience of rejection for some twenty years or more, the handicapped adult usually has built up certain protective barriers which may tend to lessen the intensity of this suffering, but it is nonetheless borne constantly within him even after several years of living in a community such as l'Arche. Scars and even open wounds remain that a lifetime may not be sufficient to erase or heal completely. Each of the handicapped at l'Arche has his own unique and poignant history of suffering, so there is hardly any point to multiplying examples. A recent incident, however, is perhaps worth recounting for its very simplicity and because to some extent it shows that even moments of joy do not exclude or erase this suffering.

At the Special Olympics for the Mentally Handicapped that took place in Paris, Jean-Charles, participating for the first time in any such competition, won a gold medal in the broad-jump. As he came down off the podium with the shining medal around his neck there were tears streaming down his cheeks. His first words to Michelle who had helped train him for the event and who was waiting to congratulate him, show that his tears were not purely tears of joy: "Now will my parents believe that I'm worth something?" In a very real way the handicapped is for most of society like the Suffering Servant of Isaiah; 53, 2-3:

> He had no form or comeliness that we should look at him, and no beauty that we should desire him. He was despised and rejected by men; a man of sorrows, and acquainted with grief; and as one from whom men hide their faces he was despised, and we esteemed him not.

Besides the experience of rejection, the other broad area of the suffering of the handicapped is that of being condemned to a life of radical dependence on others. Most of them will never be able to be sufficiently autonomous to marry and raise their own family. Their awareness of this is a source of great suffering. It is especially in this life of dependence that they experience their own human poverty. In this they are seen by many, and Père Thomas often refers to this, as the little ones, the poor in spirit of the Gospel, who because of their suffering and their dependence are very much disposed for the Good News of Salvation.

The great amount of suffering that is experienced by the assistants at l'Arche is rather more remarkable and not as easily accounted for. There is, of course, the empathy, the profound sharing in the suffering of the handicapped, but this alone does not explain why so many are seemingly at the very limit of their endurance in one way or another – physically exhausted and/or evidently suffering interiorly. This does not mean that they are dragging themselves around with long faces. Quite the contrary, as is shown by the fact that passing visitors see nothing but the joy of the community. Their tears are usually reserved for moments when they are alone or with the chaplain or an intimate friend.

The fatigue is perhaps rather easily understood. We saw that besides the more practical work of administration, supervision of workshops, housekeeping and the like, for all the assistants there is the all-important life of being present to the handicapped in a deeply personal and accepting way. They, for their part, have a real thirst for such relationships, partly because of having been so much deprived of such relationships, and partly because their limited intelligence makes them especially apt for living on the level of affections and of personal relationships. The difference, for example, between being at table with a group of so called normal people and being at table with the fellows at l'Arche is perhaps illustrative here. In the former case we may have some very stimulating, even very taxing conversation about some important political or social issue, or even about more personal aspects of our own lives, yet it usually remains little more than an exchange of ideas. On the other hand, at l'Arche with Jean-Claude, François and others there is little or no exchange of ideas. The content of our conversation is most elementary. What is most important is simply the fact that we are communicating. Their looks and their few words and gestures, or sometimes their profusion of words and gestures, have their real importance much more evidently as signs and questions of the degree to which one is accepted and loved for himself. I am forced to be present and to give of myself much more out of the depth of my person in this latter situation. This kind of relationship can be very fulfilling and joyful, but in the long run it can also be quite exhausting. Some of the assistants are with the men and women through much of their waking hours and so live constantly in this kind of intensely personal way. This explains their fatigue, and explains why many discover a great need for periods of solitude to nourish and replenish themselves in the depths of their being.

Some assistants, after spending some time at l'Arche and prior to making any kind of permanent commitment to it, go through a certain painful period of indecision. They begin to discover that l'Arche is a kind of other world of values quite different from, and in some ways opposed to, the world in which they had lived, and in which their family and many friends may still live. They begin to wonder which of these two is the "true" world. Somehow they sense that giving themselves totally to the world of l'Arche would mean to lose contact with that other world, the world of efficiency and competition, of fine clothes, restaurants and other forms of distraction. Their frequent trips into Paris are at least in part a kind of testing to see if they can still be a part of that other world. The difficulty of reinsertion for a peson leaving l'Arche indicates that this problem is not purely imaginary.

These people have discovered something very worthwhile at l'Arche, and feel an invitation or call to commit themselves more totally to l'Arche itself or at least to this kind of life-style. It is also conceived by some as a call to accept the Lord and the exigencies of his Gospel. At the same time they sense that such a commitment implies an important renunciation, a giving up of the very possibility of participating further with any kind of ease in the world symbolized by *gai Paris*. Hence, the painful state of indecision.

There is a much deeper suffering in a few of those who have already made a more total commitment to l'Arche. These are especially people in whom the personality remains yet quite unstructured by a professional training or other kinds of formation. This lack of structure means that they are extremely open and can relate to the handicapped very simply and directly as person to person without the limiting structures of educator to student, or doctor to patient, or the like. But such lack of structure also implies a defenselessness and fragility. Because they are so open and defenseless they can be easily wounded, much like the handicapped themselves. Such people, while they may have few responsibilities in the community, are extremely important. It is they who identify most completely with the handicapped and do most to create the unity between the two groups. They suffer because of their fragility and openness and sometimes because they have little experience of their usefulness in the community. It is often through a life of prayer that their affectivity is gradually assumed into an interior growth – a growth that usually involves an increasing identification with the poverty and weakness of Jesus in the crib and on the cross, and the deepening acceptance of Paul's insight that our very weakness is our strength: "because when I am weak, I am strong with the power of Christ." (2 Cor. 12,10).

In considering the organization and structure, we spoke of the insecurity in which some of the assistants are called to live. This is felt most deeply by those who are unmarried, and still undecided whether or not to choose this state as a way of life. Some, in fact, sense a real call to give themselves totally to the work and life precisely in this state of celibacy. To respond to this call is not easy in a community where men and women live in such close relationship. Yet it is especially through such intimacy that a celibate life can in fact be lived creatively. Once such a choice is made the insecurity is greatly relieved. However, it still remains a more difficult vocation than that of the consecrated religious who has declared publicly that this choice has been made. In the latter situation there is usually the support of a community either of men or of women who have made this same commitment. The vocation to celibacy in a community such as l'Arche must be daily reaffirmed. It can only be sustained by an active faith in this way of life.

This vocation to celibacy on the part of the assistants is very important. It is a source of strength and encouragement to the men and women who are condemned to it by the fact that they cannot assume the responsibility of marriage. Often it is precisely when they realize that they cannot marry this or that person whom they love that the handicapped face most deeply their human limitations. For many of them the ability to marry is the very touchstone of normalcy. Seeing those who could marry freely choosing not to, opens to the handicapped the possibility of assuming their own celibacy as a vocation.

The married vocation at l'Arche is not without its own kind of difficulty. The life there calls for such consuming presence to all those in the homes and workshops and so forth that a married couple often feels very torn. To be present and supportive to each other and to their children in this situation is a source of constant tension.

Finally, it should be noted that in some ways l'Arche rather attracts people who are fragile and who have already known considerable suffering. Such people find there the possibility of giving some meaning to their suffering. Certainly, not a few of the assistants are also "handicapped" in relationship to a competitive society that puts such emphasis on technology and efficiency. They have come to l'Arche precisely because it provides a viable alternative to a way of life which was unsatisfactory and in some cases even intolerable.

Few of the assistants, however, have come to l'Arche because they simply could not cope with "normal" society. They come for a whole variety of reasons, from the most altruistic to rather selfish motivation. They may not necessarily suffer greatly at l'Arche, but almost all if they stay long enough do come to a deeper sense of their own poverty. To be called on constantly to give of oneself in intimately personal relationships forces one to discover some of his limitations in this regard. Faced with someone who is very anguished and to discover no way of responding to him is a very humbling experience. To discover in people rejected from society as handicapped human qualities far richer than I myself possess is also a humbling experience. Such experiences are part of the daily life of l'Arche. Most assistants are sooner or later forced to realize their equality with those who are called handicapped. They are handicapped in some ways and gifted in others, and so too each one of us.

To encounter the handicapped, these "poor ones", is to come to know one's own poverty. Such an experience for a believing Christian serves to deepen his awareness of certain essential aspects of his faith. For those with little or no faith, the discovery of their own poverty can be an especially frightening experience. They sometimes try to suppress a total recognition of it, as perhaps to some extent we all do. If they do accept their equality with the handicapped, their own poverty, it is usually a first step at least towards accepting or discovering a living and loving God. There are actually not a great many formal religious conversions among the assistants who come to l'Arche. This is perhaps partly due to the fact that there is no direct work of evangelization but rather a spirit of great acceptance. It is also because in such a community of the poor one realizes with frightening forcefulness the extent to which living for God means dying to oneself. However, almost all come to a greater awareness of their need for others, and are usually better disposed to encounter the Other.

L'Arche, then, is a community of the poor in the sense of the suffering and the poor in spirit who recognize their radical poverty as human beings and their need for one another and for the Lord. The suffering and the awareness of one's poverty are powerful forces for unity in the community. Perhaps, this was most concretely manifested two years ago on the occasion of the death of Claude. Claude had been at l'Arche only a short time, but long enough to be known by all. He died unexpectedly during the night, suffocating in an epileptic fit. It was the first death in the community. The days that followed, and especially the day of his funeral, was a time of intense peace and unity. The whole event was corporately experienced as a kind of mysterious passing of the Lord. A similar experience was had when

Marie-France of Valinos died, and at Asha Niketan not along ago when Kannan, a young man who had been there only a short time, accidently drowned. On this latter occasion Gabrielle wrote to all at Trosly:

> We sense so deeply that all that took place this Monday of Pentecost is in some mysterious way the work of the Holy Spirit. How else explain this profound unity among us, after the tensions and crises of recent weeks? To the degree that God makes us enter into the mystery of death – of His Death – there is a joy so limpid, a peace so profound that inundates us. . . .

The handicapped, and this has been shown on other occasions of the death of friends and relatives, are extremely sensitive and open to the mystery of death. They live such moments with great compassion and a deep faith that death is the beginning of a new life. This is surely due to their great simplicity and heightened affectivity, but also to their own suffering. Suffering and poverty are themselves a foretaste or the seeds of death. All of us somehow vaguely sense this in our own suffering and in the suffering of others we encounter. Not only does death in the ultimate sense unite the community, but also all those minor deaths: the epileptic fits, the depressions, the tantrums and the more constant anguish and frustrations and fatigue that are so much a part of the daily life.

This unity that has its source in suffering is mostly communicated at an infra-verbal level. The handicapped often have not even verbalized to themselves much of their suffering. The assistants more commonly do not find it helpful to verbalize either their own suffering or their compassion for others. A look or a clasped hand is all that is needed to show that one understands and is united to the other in his suffering, and is often all one can muster by way of a cry for help from the depths of his own anguished heart. Words even at their best are poor vehicles of communication in this domain. Many of the assistants on first coming to l'Arche, especially the college students from North America, are baffled and rather dismayed by the silence of the more permanent assistants. It usually takes months to begin to enter more deeply into the suffering of the community and into the non-verbal communion that is a part of the spiritual unity generated by this suffering. The suffering is, both for individuals and for the community as a whole, a call towards silence and interiority – towards prayer.

The prayer life at l'Arche finds its source very especially in this suffering or poverty of spirit. There are cetainly no rules or obligations about prayer or the use of the sacraments. These are structured into the life from within, from the vital need to find support and strength in one's weakness and suffering. There are many there who feel very deeply that it is only thanks to the daily Mass and some moments of quiet in the chapel that they can get through the day. Prayer and sacraments are an existential obligation for many – not a question of rules or habit, but of survival.

The prayer life for both the handicapped and the assistants is very strongly centred on the Eucharist or Holy Communion, on a belief that they meet Jesus in a special way through the bread and wine consecrated by the priest. The concrete symbolism of the Eucharist that can be seen and touched and eaten is especially meaningful for people of great simplicity who live very much on the level of affections, and for people who are too tired or anguished to do much thinking. Both assistants and handicapped are drawn to daily worship out of a sense of their own poverty and their need and hunger for the Lord.

There are signs that indicate the reality of the faith that many of the handicapped have in the Eucharistic Presence. The very fact that so many participate when they are perfectly free not to is already indicative. Furthermore, it can be seen in the faces of many at moments during the service, especially at the consecration and communion. Many also go regularly to the Adoration (a prayer service centered around the Eucharist) on Tuesday evenings. The atmosphere during this hour in which decades of the Rosary are preceded by a few prayerful words from Père Thomas, and followed by moments of silence, is charged with a peace and concentration that makes one sense the presence of the Spirit in a way that is all but tangible. Often the handicapped will speak of Jesus' presence in the Eucharist in a way that shows how very real this presence is to them. Sometimes their words have an originality that leaves no doubt that they are not repeating someone else's words. Like André explaining to Claude, who was preparing for his first Communion, what Jesus does for him in Communion: "You know, Claude, Jesus calms your nerves." Père Thomas has discovered that the unique way of catechizing the handicapped is with relationships to the Eucharist. Furthermore, it is striking that even those who do not come to the services, will come to see Père Thomas in moments of difficulty and ask him to pray at the

Eucharist for their mother who is sick, or a relative who has died, or for whatever else might be troubling them.

Nowhere is the unity of the community more profoundly experienced than at the Eucharist. Here especially the assistants become aware that they are on a level of perfect equality with the handicapped, and the handicapped realize their equality with the assistants. In fact, here the poorest and most suffering have a place of predilection. The sermons of Père Thomas often recall Jesus' desire to receive the little ones because they are the model for a truly Christian posture: "let the little children come to me, for of such is the kingdom of Heaven." (Mt. 19, 14). Furthermore, in worshipping daily with these "poor in spirit", one becomes gradually more conscious of the fact that Jesus' privileged audience was precisely the poor and suffering. He pointed out that the very proof of His Messiahship is that: "the blind see, the lame walk ... and the poor have the gospel preached to them." (Lk. 7, 22) The intensity of the faith of many of the handicapped, their eagerness to be there close to Jesus in the Eucharist, cannot but impress anyone who comes regularly to the services. So here at worship the assistants become constantly more aware that at the profoundest level of their existence, in their relationship with God, they must strive to put on something of that childlike simplicity of these privileged ones.

Furthermore, this is true even in regard to understanding and assimilating the Gospel message. Père Thomas insists, and this is also my personal experience, that in preaching at these services one has the impression that it is precisely the handicapped who profit the most from hearing the Word of the Lord. This is also the experience of all who participate in the monthly Bible vigils or in the hour of sharing prayerfully over the text of the Gospel for the Sunday Mass. The handicapped tend to respond very directly to the Gospel, grasping what is essential without getting caught up in distracting intellectual debate. Often in these sharing sessions the assistants are reduced to a kind of awesome silence in hearing the handicapped speak out of the depths of their hearts of this Jesus who is so real and important to them and of their struggle to put His message into practice. Here it becomes clear how true are the words of Karl Rahner that God reserves to Himself the science of the heart. The Holy Spirit can and evidently does speak directly in the hearts of those who have little intellectual capacity, or in those who, in the words of John of the Cross, have "dispoiled" themselves of their reasoning and imagining powers to encounter the Lord in that direct intimacy of heart to heart. Many of the assistants come to realize, therefore, the implications of the fact that Jesus' privileged audience was the poor in spirit. They are the most apt to understand His message, and so, to better understand the Gospel, the assistants must learn from the handicapped this kind of simplicity and poverty of spirit.

So the faith dimension of the life at l'Arche is the source of a tremendously dynamic spirit in the community. The handicapped may be very seriously limited and wounded in their intelligence, nervous system and psyche. They may be incapable of doing much effective work; they may not always manifest any progress in these domains; they may even seem to regress. However, at the deepest level of their existence they are called into divine sonship, where their human limitations no longer hinder progress, and in fact seem rather to favour it. On this level there is an experience of equality and uniqueness. Each is a child of God, with his unique relationship to the Lord, and his unique relationship to the others in the community. They all need one another to progress in the Spirit, to go forward with Jesus towards the Father.

Furthermore, for the assistants to discover their radical equality with those who are in some ways the rejects of our society, is for them to have a kind of lived experience of the radical equality of all men. In discovering in the despised and rejected Jean-Charles, Claude, or Jacqueline a brother and a sister who have much to teach me both on the human and spiritual level, I realize implicitly that there is no one who should be despised and rejected. Of course, every Christian and many non-Christians believe in the Fatherhood of God and the brotherhood of all men. But it is a truth that comes alive for many at l'Arche with a certain forcefulness. If these rejected of our society are so obviously dear to the Father and such equal partners in any relationship of friendship that I might establish with them, then there is no one who is not dear to the Father and at least potentially my friend, my brother. There is a growing sense, however vague and unexplicit, among many at l'Arche that forming community with the handicapped, with the "poor", does not stop with the boundaries of Trosly or the other l'Arche centers. These are surely focal points, but the community of the poor in which one shares flows outwards to embrace the whole of suffering mankind.

The joys of l'Arche: work and play.

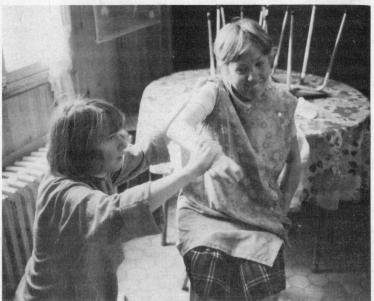

Therapy: the Free Expression workshop (*top*);
for Jacqueline at Valinos.

CHAPTER SIX

The Heart of the Matter

One of the most extraordinary aspects of the experience of l'Arche is the quality and depth of the interpersonal relationships. It is especially this experience of deep personal sharing that enables the people there to live with the amount of suffering that they do. On the other hand, it is the facing and accepting of suffering that is probably the most significant dynamic working to generate this deep level of sharing.

I personally have learned much about human relations while living at l'Arche. Perhaps no one has taught me more in this regard than a fellow I shall call David with whom I now have a very profound friendship. For two summers in a row, David and I were together at La Merci during the vacation month of August. Part of David's anguish can be traced back to the anguish and confusion of his mother, which in turn can be traced to her husband who died as a result of the cruelties suffered during his internment with the Jews in a Nazi death camp. So David is a kind of last link in a whole chain of violence. Although not a Christian, he has a deep sense of the sacred, and so he was attracted to the religious ceremonies and to me, the priest. Because of his ambivalent relationship with his mother he is unsure of who he is and quite confused as to how to receive and express feelings of affection. All this is very complex but it is not necessary to go into it. The issue that is important here is that as a result of all this David has developed some extraordinarily refined techniques for annoying people, all of which he turned on me precisely because he was attracted to me. One of these techniques was to ask the same simple questions over and over again all day long and day after day. Another was to approach you face-to-face and put his two hands around the back of your head. While saying how much he likes you he would begin jerking your head forward. Thus looking you straight in the eyes he could see just exactly how you were reacting to this treatment, and he could feel immediately to what extent you were resisting or tensing up as a result of it. Well, these are only two of a whole array of techniques by which he would desperately try to relate to others out of all his confusion and need for love, or by which at least he could give himself some reason why others do not love him. The first summer I lived with David in the close confinement of La Merci I grew to like him, but was quite beside myself as to how to handle him. Usually, I would let him go so far with his annoying tactics until I felt I just had to resist him. I would do this forcibly but with every effort to use no more force than was necessary, always trying to let him know that I still liked him. And so the month went by, with both of us growing a little in our liking for one another but with little real change in either one of us.

The second summer arrived and David took up right where he had left off eleven months earlier. I, too, began just where I had left off with him, but perhaps a bit exasperated to realize there was going to be another whole month of David's ceaseless annoyances to put up with. In any case, what I began to realize was that when I resisted him with force, the force was not totally under my control and an expression of my desire to help him. The force always controlled me to some extent, and became a subtle means of inflicting some revenge on my aggressor. . . . Also, a conversation with Jean Vanier about this time made me think out and pray about my relationship to David. Vanier was pointing out precisely that role of the assistants as one of a peaceful or non-violent presence to absorb some of the anguish of the handicapped that a life of rejection has engendered in them. I began to realize that any resistance to David was a kind of violence that only added another link to the whole chain of violence in which he was a victim. So I adopted an attitude of greater receptivity and non-violent resistance, allowing him to do as he pleased with me.

I now realize in retrospect that it was David himself who greatly helped me to adopt this attitude by his own acceptance and forgiveness of my aggression towards him. The first thing that I discovered once I stopped resisting him was that a great deal of tension went out of me. I could now adopt a very simple and consistent openness to him. The words were the same ones I had always used but they had a much fuller meaning. I was not being dishonest earlier when I told him that I liked him but to the degree that I resisted him, to that degree I was failing to accept him as he is, and was preferring my need for peace and quiet to his need for love and understanding. Now I found myself no longer avoiding his company but rather seeking him out just for the pleasure of being with him. Although nothing seemed to have changed in his attitude towards me, something had changed quite considerably in me by virtue of the gift I had received to no longer resist his aggressive activity. This gift or grace came through David himself and through the community that encourages and supports such an attitude. There were, of course, still failures in this attitude towards him but at least there was a beginning of a more unconditioned love for him and as usual David was always quick to forgive me. Now it mattered much less to me that David change. I wanted him to grow, but my love for him was not on the condition that he grow and be different than he was. I could accept him much more just as he was. In the lowering of some of my own barriers of aggression and self-preservation, the two of us came much closer together. With this greater closeness I could see much more of the goodness and beauty of his person, which one could scarcely fail to love.

It neither surprised nor disappointed me that there was no immediate change in David's conduct. What did surprise me was that after a couple of weeks he went into a very quiet, reflective mood, during which time he ceased all his annoying habits. In fact, he simply avoided people. This lasted a few days, but then when he began coming out of this mood and being more himself there was still a very striking change in him. His annoying tactics were greatly reduced and he seemed to have made a real step forward in being able to relate to people more simply and directly. It is not my intention here to analyse what took place in David's experience. It could well be that his change in attitude was brought on by factors other than that of his relationship to me. In any case we have each done much to heal and to free one another, but the issue at hand is primarily the change that took place in myself.

This friendship has taught me something about myself and my limitations in accepting others. In helping me to lower some of the barriers which separated us, David has led me to a greater awareness of the ways I keep others at a distance and refuse to allow them to be themselves. Allowing him to be more himself enabled me to be more myself. It is clear that the acceptance of others is a direct function of the acceptance of oneself. The more I accept myself the more I can accept others, and the more I accept others the more I can accept myself. This acceptance becomes increasingly more difficult in a community that seeks its unity through some sort of conformity or uniformity, rather than through the complementation of the uniqueness of each of its members. The tremendously rich potential in friendships, marriages, parental relationships, religious communities, teacher-student relations, and in many other human relationships is often never brought to any kind of fulfillment precisely because of this desire to make the other conform rather than to allow him to be in all his uniqueness.

Man's natural drive for self-preservation leads him to construct an array of barriers to protect himself from others. Some of these barriers are in fact necessary for survival, but barriers not only keep outsiders from getting in, they also keep insiders from getting out. So, the barriers we construct become in some ways our own prisons or coffins. The reasons for constructing these barriers are of course multiple and complex, but certainly a great deal of it has to do with our fear of being wounded or rejected, that is, of being diminished or even destroyed. So latent in most of these fears is the fear of death itself. This helps to explain why there is so much fear and rejection of such innocent and harmless people as Denis and David and others who have been deeply wounded either physically, psychically or socially. These people bear in such an evident way the signs of death. So, the natural tendency is to treat them as non-persons. They are not persons to know and love but patients to be placed in institutions, or problems to be resolved by social legislation. My fear of the down-and-outer who asks me for a dime is not primarily a financial issue. Often, even in conceding to his request, I dare not look into his eyes but simply look away or look through him with a kind of stare that says, "I want nothing to do with this *thing,* but just want to get it out of my way as quickly as possible." I cannot allow him to be a person, because a person is what I am. If he is a person, then in some way we are equal and he mirrors to me something of myself. He is a "dying" man and so my fear of death prevents me from seeing him as a man at all for fear of seeing in him my own death.

Our freedom to be ourselves depends on our freedom to accept others because it is only in relationship to other persons that the human person can blossom. So in many ways the greatest freedom comes in accepting the seemingly most unacceptable, those who most evidently manifest the signs of death.

This kind of freedom is not easily achieved in a technological society, where the value of interpersonal relationships is often lost in the shadow of the supreme value of efficiency imposed by the laws of economy and competition. Production then seems to become an end in itself rather than a means to human fulfillment, and individuals are valued only in terms of their capacity to produce. In a society with these criteria, the handicapped have no place. They must be rejected as useless. Production is also important at l'Arche, but it does not become an end in itself. Here even the work becomes the means by which personal relationships are enhanced.

This latter truth is quickly grasped by a visit to l'Arche's central office at Trosly. This seems more like a coffee house than an office. The moment you meet Barbara, Jean Vanier's "secretary" (the term is inadequate since she fills a multiplicity of roles and seems to embody the very spirit of l'Arche), it is obvious that you are a long way from a General Motors-type enterprise. Barbara's attire reflects the disorder of the office itself, but her joy and personal warmth usually distract people from paying much attention to this. The office is faithful to what it is called, *l'acceuil*, which means the place of welcome. It was my personal experience that when I was tired and in need of a lift it was usually to the office that I would gravitate. A great number of people pass through the office each day. Besides administrators from other centres, business men, parents of the handicapped, heads of workshops and homes, and other visitors, many of the handicapped come and go. They either come to meet the visitors, or unburden themselves of some particular anguish, or simply to laugh with Barbara and the others who share the secretarial load with her. The phone rings constantly, and when the one who answers lets out an "Alleluia!" it is a sure sign that the call is from one of the other l'Arche centers elsewhere in France, or on rare occasions from elsewhere in the world. This usually precipitates a kind of explosion of joy, and many will come to the phone to exchange a few loving words besides Jean Vanier or Miss Maurice or whoever else may be dealing with the matter of business for which the call was made. To make oneself at home in the office one must usually clear a place.

Mounds of letters and other papers are piled on desks and chairs with photos, books on poetry or mysticism, cakes and cheese and perhaps a half-emptied bottle of wine or cognac. Vanier often encourages Barbara to put some order into the place, but it only brings limited results for the briefest periods of time. But in spite of all the chaos the business of organizing meetings, writing letters, translation of Vanier's articles and books from French to English or from English to French somehow gets done. This is largely due to the fact that in the quiet of the small hours of the morning Barbara is still happily at work.

The significance of the work for the handicapped might be best understood by assisting at one of the meetings when they and the assistants get together to discuss the work. On the last Friday of each month there is a reunion of all the handicapped and those who assist them in the workshops, gardens, and other areas of work. Michel, who is in charge of all the work, chairs the meeting. Last Friday's meeting was a fairly typical one. The meeting was scheduled to begin at 4:45. By 4:30 the room is already half full, and charged with an atmosphere of friendship and joy like that of group of young people preparing for a folk Mass or a rock festival. By 4:45 the room is packed with about eighty people, including about fifteen assistants.

Michel is sitting towards the front at one end of the semi-circle of people crowded together on chairs or on the floor. The room becomes somewhat quieter as he begins to speak. The atmosphere of joyful seriousness, and of great respect shown by Michel and everyone towards whatever anyone has to say is not easy to express. However, perhaps some of this will come through in the parts of the meeting that I will now present in a rough translation.

Michel (M): Well, let's see. This makes how many times we have gotten together?

Several People (S.P.): (shouting out spontaneously) Two! Five! Many! Eight!

M: Let's just see, now. We began in October. That makes (he counts them out on his fingers, and several of the boys say the months with him) October, November, December, January, and now February. So this is our fifth meeting. O.K. . . . ?

S.P.: Yes! O.K. Michel! O.K.!

M: And who can tell us why it is we have these meetings?

Jean-Paul: To consider the problems of the workshops.

Michel F: To see what is being done in the different workshops.

André: (bursting with the desire to speak but not knowing what to say) Ah . . . for the work. Ah . . . to discuss things. Ah . . .

Claude: To talk about our work.

M: Good. So let's begin by seeing how things are going in the different areas of work. Let's start with the mosaics. Can someone from the mosaics give us a report?

Benoit: (raising his hand and shouting) Me!

M: O.K., Benoit, go ahead.

Benoit: (In a rapid mechanical tone, and stopping as abruptly as he begins) I'm making a clown!

M: Thank you, Benoit. Now what else is being done in the mosaics . . . . Jean-Paul, can you carry on?

Jean-Paul: (with a very evident pride) Well, Benoit is making a clown, but we are doing all kinds of different designs: clowns, birds, the Blessed Virgin, and other things. And different kinds of things: for hanging on the walls, or putting on the table under serving dishes, tables . . . We just sold a big table – one of those with the wrought-iron frame that George and Marcel made in the ironworks shop. Things are going really well. There is just one problem. Michel T. plays his transistor too loud.

M: Good. Now we've already spoken about this business of the transistors. O.K. Michel?

Michel T: (Scratching his head, and pushing up his glasses, he tries to smile, and mumbles a reply) Yes, O.K.

M: Is there anyone who does not want any transistors in the workshops? Is there anyone who finds this annoying?

S.P.: No! No problem! No!

M: Fine. Obviously no one should play his transistor so loud that it bothers people. Is everyone agreed about this?

S.P.: O.K.! Agreed! Yes!

The two boys who reported on the mosaics seem to be such different people that it is hard to imagine them working together in the same shop. They are both blond and fairly tall, but here the resemblance ceases. Benoit seems to be off in his own little world, with little sense of the people around him. Jean-Paul shows little or no signs of being handicapped. He has an extraordinary presence. He is very well groomed and expresses himself very correctly. Evidently, however, making mosaics responds to a certian need or desire in both these young men. They are both very happy to be there.

In this particular workshop, each person works on his own so there is no problem in having people of very different capacities working here. Perhaps it is this that most marks this workshop – a spirit of quiet and concentration. Most of the eight or nine who work here will look up and give you a smile as you come through the door, but then at least half of them will return to cutting and gluing the pieces of ceramic that go to make up the mosaic. Jean-Michel will almost certainly come over to greet you, rolling up his sleeve as he comes. He will welcome you with overly gracious words, and take your hand and place it on his bare forearm and hold it there firmly. If you are a stranger he will ask you if this bothers you, and, in any case, he will keep up a flow of converstion in order to hold onto your hand as long as possible. Meanwhile you might get him to show you his work. Usually it is a large and complicated design, which he executes with extraordinary finesse. He is evidently proud of his work, even though he finds every possible excuse to avoid doing it. When you get your hand back from Jean-Michel you might offer it to Tiery, who works next to him. Tiery may respond with a brief and feeble handshake but will more commonly just look at your hand and then turn away. Only gradually will he look at you with a furtive glance, and maybe finally a smile, or a laugh, but whether this is in friendship or mockery is not quite evident. Tiery has great difficulty concentrating on his work. He will hold a piece of ceramic in his hand for maybe ten minutes, looking at it, looking around the room, perhaps smiling to himself before he finally glues it rather carelessly to the simple little mosaic that he may have been working on for a month or more. Philippe, next to Tiery, will be overjoyed to greet you and show you with great pride the work he is doing. He might quickly turn the conversation to the film he saw last night on TV, or to his slide collection and a request that you help him procure some slides from your part of the country or the world. Philippe expresses himself very articulately but with his own unique logic, that is not always easy to follow. Claude and Michel, who work side by side, are evidently close friends. They spend much time conversing but without ceasing to continue their work. Claude produces work of excellent quality. From time to time he pushes back his chair, takes his harmonica and plays a few tunes that express something of his own peace and joy. Michel's work is hampered by his very bad eyesight, but he is happy to be doing this rather artistic type of work and is proud of his accomplishments. In the corner but facing towards the center of the room is Abdullah. He cannot speak, but he will welcome you with a warm smile. He might begin to extend his left hand to you, but then, with a smile, and a bit of an effort offer you his slightly crippled right hand. Since beginning to do some physical therapy one afternoon a week, Abdullah is making more of an effort to use his crippled right side. He will nod and grunt yes or no in response to your questions, but most of all he will simply smile and let you know by this that he is pleased to have you watch him work – something he does with great slowness and awkwardness but with very fine results. The two or three assistants who work in this shop will also greet you warmly, but then continue their work of designing or tracing out the patterns to be made, or looking after the accounts, or seeing to the minimum of supervision that is necessary. They are content to leave the business of public relations to Jean-Paul or Jean-Michel, who are more than happy to welcome visitors and show them around.

The atmosphere in this shop is usually one of quiet order, except for the moments that Tiery takes it in his head to pour glue in Lucy's hair, and, with a fiendish glint in his eye, chases her around the room until someone rescues her. The peace is also occasionally disturbed by a violent outburst when the usually gentle Abdullah loses his temper at someone, which is more an expression of his frustration at not being able to talk than something he really has against the person concerned. However, what is most impressive about this and most of the other workshops is the way the people accept one another, the prevailing spirit of joy, and their manner of making you feel welcome when you visit them.

Having received the report from the mosaics and having settled the difficulty about the use of transistors, Michel goes on to ask for reports from the other workshops.

M: Well, let's hear from the workshop that is doing the lamps (assembling and packing them for a nearby plastic factory). Can someone tell us how things are going here?

Michel F: It's going great. We did a lot more this week than last.

Alain: (the assistant in charge of all the work done for the factories) I was at the factory yesterday. They are very pleased with our work, and have promised to give us a great deal more to do. In a month's time we will be handling between sixty and seventy per cent of all their production.

M: That's great. Did you all understand what Alain just said. (He goes on to explain this in very simple terms.)

M: Now the *bouchons* (the workshop that assembles the plastic bushings for the same factory). Yes, Jenny's workshop. (Jenny is a young Canadian who supervises, or rather, works along with the men in this workshop.)

Pierre: We are now working on an assembly line. It seems to be going well but I'd like to know how many we did this week.

Alain: I can't give you the figures yet, but Monday morning I'll let each workshop know what its production was for this week. O.K.?

M: And the others, how is the work going?

André: (Again, bursting with a desire to speak but now knowing what to say) Ah. . . . yes. It's going O.K.

Patrick: (with a huge smile) I'm working hard!

M: And you, Jean-Charles?

Jean-Charles: (who mumbles inarticulately) ya. . . . O.K.

M: Let's admit that you are not very often on the job, Jean-Charles.

Jean-Charles: (protesting but with no sign of embarrassment) Ah, no!

M: The work is going so well for our friend Jean-Charles that he spends most of the day walking around the village to tell everybody about it.

(Everyone bursts into laughter, including Jean-Charles himself.)

M. And how are things going in the *Sac en papier* (folders for storing archives or filing letters and notes). Robert, who just arrived last week?

Robert: (Nodding but seeming to be too shy to speak.)

Jacques: (Standing and assuming a very business-like attitude.) We really turned in a day's work today, we made 350. It started a bit slow this morning. The fellows on the forms (the first operation in this small assembly line) were not on the ball this morning, but they sure turned it on this afternoon, and more than made up for it.

M: Yes, we'll have to admit that the fellows on the forms really worked, eh, Patrick, eh George? (Patrick and George are all smiles.)

Finally they go on to consider how the work is going in the gardens, on the maintenance crew, and for those who help out in the kitchens of the different houses. Then Michel goes on to introduce another matter.

M: That's fine, now we want to discuss the important question of salaries. We have already discussed before why the pay for each month is delayed. (They all receive a small pay each Friday, plus a larger sum once a month.) You know that all the money that comes in from the sale of mosaics, the folders, ironwork, and from the work that you do for the factories all comes back to you in salaries. Now the factories don't pay us right away for our work. The way they run their accounts, they can't pay us right away, but only about six weeks later. So it will only be next Monday, the 20th, that you will receive your monthly pay, and it is for the work you did during the month of December. Do you all understand this? (Many nod their assent.) Fine, so who can repeat what I just said?

Roland: Yes! Me! (He wants so much to be able to say

something but has obviously not understood a word of what has been said.) Ah...Ah...Ah...

Michel F: (taking over for Roland) You said that the factories are six weeks behind in paying for our work...ah ...and that we will get paid on Monday.

Pierre: I've another question. What about this business of half of our salaries being taken away from us?

M: Good. I've explained this before but it's good that you bring it up again. That's right, half of each person's salary goes in to help pay for his food, lodging and the like. You see, a good deal of money is spent for these things, and it seems right, doesn't it, that you should help share these costs? This is important, so I hope everyone understands this.

S.P.: Yes. Yes, Michel. O.K.

George: (A big fellow in blue cover-alls, who has been standing rather sullenly at the back just inside the door.) No, I don't agree.

M: What is it you don't agree with, George?

George: I don't agree that half our pay should be taken and given to those who don't work.

M: But, George, you haven't understood Pierre's question. That's not the issue. Pierre, can you explain this to George?

After a few exchanges George seems to be reassured. Part of his difficulty was a newly-inaugurated system of grading them into four different categories according to their capacities to work. Michel then goes on to explain that he will be happy to discuss individually any difficulties that people might have with their own salaries. He stresses the fact that this is a private affair that he does not want to discuss in a public meeting like this. At this point Jean raises his hand and asks just such a question: why is it that he received only four and a half francs this week, instead of the usual five? Michel begins again, with great patience, to explain that just such questions should be handled privately. Jean, continues to insist, until he is finally made to see that he will have to see Michel later in his office. Several other issues are discussed, and finally, when there are no more questions, the meeting is adjourned. Instantly, Jean-Claude, as is his custom, jumps to his feet singing Alleluia. A few others join in the singing, or burst into noisy bantering and laughter, while others cluster in small groups to "rehash" what has been said during the hour and a quarter. The meeting ends as happily as it began.

The spirit that pervades such meetings as well as that which reigns in the workshops and other areas of work is enough to show something of the importance that their work has in the lives of these men. This is certainly verified by Michel himself, and others who are responsible for this aspect of the life at Trosly. The satisfaction of being able to work is in itself of tremendous importance for these people who, prior to coming to l'Arche, have never been able to have a steady job. You sense immediately upon entering any one of the workshops that these people are not working just because they need money, or because they are being forced to work. It is, for almost all of them, a joy to be able to work. One of the things they often will mention in saying why they are happy to be at l'Arche, is precisely the fact that here they can work. This would explain, too, why little Patrick could say to me as he did last Saturday, that he will be happy when the week-end is over and he can go back to work.

None of this is to deny that some, from time to time, have to be cajoled into going to work. Others cannot stay at their job unless there is an assistant beside them constantly to encourage them. On the other hand, some will not want to stop working and will have to be told to stop. Like Joseph, who works in the gardens and especially likes cleaning up the flower beds, rose bushes and the like. The only problem being that, if one does not pay close attention to him, when Joseph is finished the flowers and rose bushes are also finished, and nothing is left but the good clean earth. Or like Daniel, who works with the maintenance crew. One day while working on a newly-purchased house, Daniel finished the job he was given of scraping the old plaster off the walls. What next? He had to keep working but there was no one to tell him what to do. He had heard that l'Arche had bought the adjacent property, which was separated by a brick wall. When Ken arrived two hours later, Daniel was just taking the last swing with his pick at what used to be a brick wall, in order that not a stone be left upon a stone. It was aesthetically and practically a fine thing to have joined the two properties. The only problem being that the adjacent property had not as yet been purchased.

In spite of the occasional error, such as this one which left Daniel very disheartened for two days, working gives the handicapped a sense of their own worth. In this regard, the salary they receive is important, not just because they need or want to have money but also because it gives a value to their work that it otherwise would not have. Some months ago four or five men went on strike to protest for higher wages. The main reason for their protest was not simply that they wanted more money to buy things, but rather a feeling that the work they were doing was worth more than they were receiving for it. Such a protest is a sign that they are achieving a certain freedom and independence and a greater sense of the value of their work.

There is, then, a way of speaking of progress with regard to the work. It is actually a progress in the people themselves, a gaining of a sense of self-worth in being able to produce, to do something deserving of praise, and deserving of a salary. Also, it is important for them to have money that they have earned themselves. Lucien recently purchased a tape-recorder for which he had been saving money for over a year. The sense of achievement in having managed to save that much money and make this purchase on his own seemed to give him far more pleasure than the tape-recorder itself. It means much to these people who have been forced to live in such total dependence on others to be able to buy their own cigarettes or pay their own way with others. There are some who will buy cookies and candies primarily just to have something to give to others. Others, like René, who loves to smoke and who earns only enough to buy a couple of packs of cigarettes a week yet will nevertheless be quick to offer cigarettes to his companions at work or at table.

With regard to their abilities and capacities to work, the term progress has much less significance. There is the occasional person who does make some remarkable progress. Like Michel P., who seemed to be very retarded when he arrived at l'Arche, but who soon began to find himself in the workshops. In a little over a year he was working in a factory, while still living at Trosly, and by the end of another year he had left l'Arche altogether to live a fairly independent existence. However, for the majority, no such progress is realized. In fact, for a few slightly older men who have been at l'Arche almost from the beginning, there would seem to be a certain regression in their productive capacity. This, of course, is no indication that l'Arche is failing these people. It is not a school or a training centre, but a community where the handicapped can, if they wish, live out their entire lives. So there will be those who do stay and live through the period of decline that comes with age, and/or with psychological regression.

So with regard to the work of the handicapped at l'Arche there is a certain inevitable element of stagnation. This is felt rather acutely at times by some of them, especially those who are perhaps less handicapped and more aware of their situation. Here comes to mind a fellow who has been at l'Arche for over five years. Let us call him Charles. Charles has been in the same workshop for four years. Now twenty-seven years old, he realizes that it is unlikely that he will ever be capable of assuming a more challenging work than this. This means that he probably will never be capable of assuming the responsibilities of marriage or even a more independent life. He is struggling to accept this reality, but finds it very painful. At times he is submerged in a state of anguish and depression. In some ways, there is nothing unique in this situation. Almost every adult sooner or later passes through the crisis of realizing that a certain limit has been reached with regard to their capacities or productivity and creativity. How many men in business, for example, at the age of about forty come to the painful realization that they have nothing more to look forward to but the moment of retirement. However, the crisis can be especially difficult for those in whom the productive and creative capacities are especially limited.

The assistants at l'Arche, depending on the degree of their sensibility and capacity for empathy, to a greater or lesser degree suffer through such crises and more permanent states of anguish with the handicapped. The anguish of Charles, for example, becomes the anguish also of those assistants who are close to him. In some ways this is precisely the essential work of the assistants, to be present to assume or absorb some of the anguish of those who are suffering from wounded intellects and nervous systems, and from the life of rejection which these wounds have incited. This aspect of the work of the assistants of its very nature entails considerable suffering and unites them to the handicapped in a very unique way, that is by compassion. This word compassion here must be taken in its literal sense, *to suffer with*. It is not a question of pity, but of entering into the other, of trying to resonate with him. Sometimes the person in question will not be able to speak, or may speak with a logic that is unique to him, that really is a kind of symbolic language, by which he is struggling to express something of his inner self, his suffering, his love, his meaning. The role of the assistant is to be present to him, with a deep respect for his person, a respect he has every right to but may never have received. It demands on the part of the assistant a real sense of the dignity of the human person and sufficient interiority to, as Vanier once put it, "hear the music of the other," to appreciate the other in all his uniqueness and try to understand and love him precisely in and for this uniqueness.

Certainly, there are more pragmatic aspects of the work of the assistants: the cooking, the housekeeping, the running of the workshops, nursing, administration and so forth. For some of the assistants this more pragmatic aspect may be predominant, and be the essential way in which they achieve a sense of self-worth. Those who do not find their place on this level are usually somewhat lost and suffer from a feeling of uselessness. Nevertheless, the primary work at l'Arche for all the assistants is to help the handicapped by creating with them a community of mutual respect and genuine friendship. There are those who do not share in the domestic life and leisure, nor in the worship of l'Arche, or perhaps in only one or another of these aspects: who work their eight hours a day, five days a week, but spend the rest of their time with their families either in the village or elsewhere. But even these people would scarcely be able to continue working at l'Arche if there were not something more than their salaries attracting them. For example, the nurse must do more than simply hand out pills. She must also communicate a certain element of gratuity, a gift of self that goes beyond whatever particular professional services or talents one might have to offer. There is hardly any way of avoiding a certain gift of self because the handicapped, who live so much on the level of affectivity, call forth this gift from those who live with them. To be called upon constantly to give of oneself might at times be almost unbearable, but it would be even more unbearable to try to live at l'Arche while refusing to give something of oneself. This issue of gift of self and of compassion touches the very heart of l'Arche.

To get a better indication of what is involved in the matter of personal relationships with the handicapped we are going to consider in some detail a particular institution at l'Arche which brings the assistants together to reflect upon this very issue.

Every Wednesday afternoon at Trosly there is a meeting of all the interested assistants to study the progress of an individual or of a certain aspect of the life and work. This meeting is under the joint guidance of the psychiatrist and Jean Vanier or, in his absence, the second in charge. It has come to be known as the *synthèse* because it culminates with the psychiatrist's attempt to synthesize the mass of information and experiences contributed by the assistants during the course of the meeting.

Since the beginning, l'Arche has had the assistance of a psychiatrist from the huge mental hospital of Clermont. This has been particularly important since many of the men and women have come to l'Arche from this hospital. The psychiatrist for the past four years has been Dr. Franko. He spends one day a week at Trosly, seeing a number of the men and women individually, and conferring with Anne-Marie, the resident psychologist, Paule and Annie, the nurse and assistant nurse, and Catherine and Thérèsè, the social workers. Finally, Dr. Franko, as was mentioned, is present for the *synthèse* to help the assistants better understand the men and women and their personal relationship to them. It is perhaps significant enough to mention that Dr. Franko is not a professing Christian. At first, this fact tended to threaten some of the assistants for whom the religious aspect of l'Arche is particularly important. It may still threaten a few people, but this is not detectable. What I have observed is a growing mutual acceptance, so that today Franko seems to be very much a part of l'Arche, a participating member of the community. The fact that he is not a Christian gives the Christians a certain sense of confidence that their attitude towards the men and women with regard to religion is being checked by an impartial observer. This is important because the handicapped are in a position of considerable dependency, so that it would be easy to violate their personal freedom in this matter.

I asked Franko what he considered to be the significance of l'Arche. An initial response, he said, is very easy to give. To take people out of such asylums as are the mental hospitals, or out of very unfortunate family situations, and to bring them into this atmosphere of respect and acceptance – obviously this is an unquestionable good. It is, he continued, like asking whether it would have been a good thing to save the Jews from the Nazi camps and ovens.

Often I have heard the men and women themselves speak of the significance of l'Arche for them. They express themselves in such terms as: here we are happy, here we have friends, here I am free and can come and go as I like, I am at home here, and so forth. Many also stress how good it is to be able to work, rather than just sit around the house all day as they did before coming to l'Arche. For others, it is to work and get paid for it. One of the boys once told me with great contentment "C'est la première fois que je suis capable de rendre service" (It's the first time I've been able to do something for others.) One day in a small group that meets weekly to pray and study the Scriptures, Jean Vanier asked Dédé what is the meaning of the word peace that Jesus was offering to his disciples the evening of His Resurrection. After a moment of reflection André responded: "La paix, c'est d'être ici." (Peace is being here at l'Arche.)

Dr. Franko then went on to consider at a second level the significance of l'Arche, and here the response is not so easy. Supposing, he continued with his example, that you save a Jew from Dachau and then bring him to this country and you put him in a house saying, "This is the house of the Jews, from now on this is where you live." This would be simply another manifestation of the same racism, and an imprisonment of another sort. Applying the example to Trosly, he noted how, for example, Raphael, in the six years he has been at l'Arche, has really blossomed as a person. He has become a very happy man, filled with a peace and a radiance which he had never known before, and a source of much happiness for others. Everyone knows him – smiling, pipe in mouth or in hand, speaking and gesturing about getting married or going dancing or the other three of four topics he constantly raises. That is Raphael. It is how we all see him, and, in a sense, that is how we may be forcing him to remain, whether he likes it or not. The problem is to be able to continue respecting Raphael's uniqueness and freedom, to continue letting him be himself, to remain open to the possibility that he can surprise us. Franko went on to illustrate what he was getting at by taking as an example an airplane's breaking the sound barrier. We had had a big discussion about this with some of the boys at lunch that day. Each time a plane's speed doubles the speed of sound it must once again break through the sound barrier. Applying this to our discussion, he noted that to bring a man to l'Arche is like breaking through the sound barrier at Mach 1, that is, for the first time. To come to l'Arche is to break through the barrier of rejection and constraint that has confined him, and to give him a new freedom to be himself. As this autonomy and personal growth develops, those who are here to help him come to know him and to expect certain things from him. One arrives at Mach 2 (twice the speed of sound), and another barrier must be broken through. Can the assistants continue respecting the uniqueness and mystery of this person to the point of allowing him to continue developing according to his own uniqueness and inner needs? Can they allow him to continue changing, to be free enough to surprise them, and even to change in ways that may make him ever more different than themselves and perhaps to the point of no longer needing their assistance? The problem here, Franko points out, is that some of the assistants might need the mentally handicapped precisely as mentally handicapped. They might, because of their own psychological needs, *have to have* this "helpless person" who depends on them. If this is the case, they cannot break through this second barrier, they cannot give the man or woman sufficient freedom to continue growing and to become independent.

The obvious question that follows is, to what extent does l'Arche in fact break through this second barrier? To what extent do the assistants respect the uniqueness and freedom of the handicapped and continue helping them to become independent? We have seen that many of those who have been at l'Arche consider one of its most enriching aspects to be precisely an atmosphere of great respect for the human person. They spoke about the liberty given to the men and women, and of their freedom to be themselves. Many mentioned how being at l'Arche deepened their own respect for the human person, and enabled them to be more truly themselves. This is a vague indication that to some extent the second barrier is being broken through. Dr. Franko, however, did not see the value in speaking in general terms. He feels that such generalities tell us only very little. This question of one's respect for the uniqueness of the other person is such a personal issue that it can only be considered in terms of each individual concerned. It is the unique problem of each assistant at l'Arche and his relation with each of the men and women and with the other assistants. The individual alone can discover to what extent he is achieving this kind of respect for the other.

One important role of Dr. Franko, which he exercises especially during the *synthèse*, is to help the assistants to become more aware of their own attitude towards the handicapped and the degree to which they actually are respecting the uniqueness and inner freedom of each one.

Let us go back to a particular Wednesday a couple of years ago when the *synthèse* was on a lad that we will, for the sake of his privacy, call by the pseudonym Paul. Since his arrival at Trosly in 1965, Paul has lived in the Val Fleuri where Gilbert is the head of the household, so it is Gilbert that presents his dossier.

Gilbert begins by noting that Paul's relationship to his family is of very great importance so that it is necessary to first look at this in some detail. As Gilbert's presentation continues it is sometimes amplified or clarified by Gerry who has been especially responsible for contacting Paul's family and trying to improve these relationships. Others, too, have information to contribute in this regard. When Paul was two or three years old his mother went off, leaving her mentally handicapped husband to care for Paul and his younger brother. Paul speaks rarely of his mother, but says that she lived not far away in an old shack, but he never wanted to see her. He was very attached to his father, who was, he says, like a mother to him. The sister of the father was also there at times to help out, but this aunt showed little love for Paul. She greatly favoured his brother. She would only very rarely, in recent years, allow Paul to come and spend a few hours at her home, and never to stay the night. Paul's father died last summer in the hospital where he had been a patient for several years. His aunt did not trouble to inform him of his father's death until a couple of months later, and this by the mediation of a third person.

After this question of family relations was further developed and clarified, Jean Vanier began to speak about Paul's progress since coming to l'Arche. He pointed out that during the first two years Paul was extremely difficult, seeming to take pleasure in attacking those weaker than himself. His attitude manifested a great interior anguish. His first reaction to any proposal was always a very sharp and definite negative response. He rejected all authority. There was a certain ambivalence shown in the fact that he often tried to hurt those for whom he had some affection. Once he had a great dispute with one of the other men in the house, and went after him with a knife. On two other occasions of great anger he lost consciousness and became as stiff and hard as a board. These were manifestations of his tremendous fear. He is especially afraid to put his feelings into action, because, as he says, he feels he has the force to kill someone. Vanier went on to note how this anguish and fear has gradually subsided. He pointed out that Paul really smiled for the first time two years after his arrival. It was his twenty-first birthday. During dinner Vanier gave a little speech, saying how much he liked Paul and how content he was to live with him. Paul was deeply moved by such acceptance. He explained later to Vanier that he had not smiled before because when he was young no one had taught him how to smile. But much fear remains. He is also afraid of being misunderstood, and afraid of being considered as a crazy person. In this respect it was mentioned how much importance he attached to an experience of last summer, when he spent the month of vacation with about thirty others from Trosly at the newly-formed community of La Merci. What meant so much to Paul during this month were the relations he and the others were able to have with the neighbours and the people of the surrounding villages. These relations were very good, and natural. He was not treated as being a bit "different".

As the *synthèse* continued it became increasingly evident that the acceptance and affection that Paul was receiving at l'Arche had helped him to achieve a quite extraordinary progress. Besides having the security of food and shelter, Paul was at least beginning to experience some satisfaction of his basic psychological needs. The home-like situation was especially responding to the need to love and to be loved. The other two fundamental needs: to produce or create, and to understand and give meaning to one's existence are to some extent being met in other ways.

Paul is, in fact, very much "at home" at the Val Fleuri. The assuring presence of Gilbert has been especially important in this regard as well as the assuring presence at Trosly of Jean Vanier. Although the woman of the house has changed three or four times, her presence, too, has been of great importance. Ginette, who is presently in charge of the house spoke of Paul's love for music and his sensitivity to others. Paul often goes to his room and plays a particular record that he knows Ginette especially likes. He turns up the volume so that she can hear it downstairs in the kitchen. When his friend Robert was sick, he was very much upset and played some very gentle music to try and soothe both Robert and himself. Frank, a young assistant from Canada shares a room with Paul. He spoke of Paul's great attachment to his room, his great care in decorating it and keeping it clean, his desire to have people come and admire it, and his fear of people entering it in his absence. Others attached to this particular home spoke of Paul's possessiveness with regard to the entire house.

103

He reserves the right to change pictures or move furniture, but cannot accept the slightest change initiated by anyone else. This fear of change over which he has no control was brought out in other aspects as well. It became clearer that, while the home situation was meeting certain needs and had enabled Paul to make great progress, there was also the risk that it become too much a "cozy nest" in which he was too secure, thus limiting the possibility of further progress.

The *synthèse* continued with the comments of other assistants who have relationships to Paul outside of the home situation. His relationship with two women assistants has been of particular importance. One of them meets with him once a week for lessons in reading, writing and arithmetic. The other has seen him more on the level of work and leisure. In both these relationships were brought out the difficulties he has in knowing how to relate to women. They mentioned his rages of jealousy when he had to share his teacher with another pupil, or when she commented on the attractiveness of the dress worn by her associate.

Next, those who were responsible for Paul with regard to his work with the garden crew, spoke of his work and what progress was being made in this respect. It was noted that he could not work in a team but had to have jobs that he could do alone. He is evidently quite proud of his work, which is giving him a greater sense of his own worth. His inability to easily accept the authority of the assistant in charge of this work crew seems to be his fear of being placed on the level of the other handicapped. Much more was said about this problem of trying to situate himself with regard to the other men and the assistants, his questioning of who he is – "handicapped or normal"? It became somewhat evident that while his work had been a great source of progress, here too the possibility of further progress was in question. This further progress seems to hinge especially on his problem of knowing who he is.

The need to understand and give meaning to his life is perhaps the psychological need that is presently most critical in Paul's life. This became more evident in the *synthèse* as Anne-Marie gave her report on the psychological tests she had recently given to Paul, and the comparison of these results with earlier tests. Other than the fact that Paul's IQ is rated at 65, the results of the several tests outlined were understood only by Dr. Franko, Jean Vanier, and one or two other assistants with some technical training in psychology. However,

Anne-Marie went on to explain in laymen's terms some of the significance of these tests. She pointed out Paul's uncertainty with respect to his own sexuality. She also observed a certain levelling-off of progress towards greater maturity, which she feared could move towards regression if they were not careful. Here again it is a question of his being able to achieve a greater independence by daring to draw away from the shelter and protection that have been so helpful for the growth he has achieved in recent years. But it is particularly a matter of resolving the question of who he is. She mentioned a frequent nightmare that Paul has. It consists of someone threatening to enter his room. This threatening person finally does get into the room and comes and opens Paul's stomach.

Finally, Dr. Franko tried to bring together into some unified picture the various things that had been presented throughout the *synthèse*. It is not important for our purpose here to outline in detail this synthesis. The main lines of it are perhaps already evident. There was the absence of Paul's mother or anyone to replace her in the home as a maternal image. The father was more mother than father. Also, the father was himself mentally handicapped, and so in some way presented more the image of child than parent. So Paul has not had the normal triangular relationship to a maternal and paternal image to come to know who he is, even with regard to the fundamental issue of his sexuality. So his fundamental problem is trying now, at the age of twenty-four, to discover who he is, in the way that is usually resolved at a very early age. His relations with the various people at l'Arche is founded on this question of his identity. In some way or other he is asking these people to tell him who he is, or to tell him who they are so that he can know who he is in relation to them.

This helps to explain some of the incidents mentioned earlier in the *synthèse*. For example, consider his anger when his teacher said to another girl that she was wearing a nice dress. More commonly both these girls have the habit of wearing slacks. Paul cannot accept that these friends be purely and simply feminine. Everything is confused: masculine or feminine? His nightmare is an expression both of the desire and the fear to discover what is inside him, to discover who he really is. All his crises hinge around this problem of his identity. It is a problem that the assistants can help him with, but which ultimately only he can resolve.

As Franko goes on, he is occasionally interrupted by demands for further explanations or by contributions of further information that might clarify his theory. Once he is finished there is a silence that seems to say, "that's a fine theory which seems to fit the facts, but what are we to do about it, how does it help us to help Paul?" This is the burden of the question that is immediately posed by Anne, the girl who does the cooking at the Val Fleuri. She points out that Paul spends a great deal of time poking around the kitchen, often criticizing her work, but also saying often enough how much he likes her. What should be her response to him? Franko points out that in saying that he likes her, Paul is posing a question, without really knowing what the response might be or by what title it might be given. He has often told this girl, who is a year younger than himself, that his affection for her is like Jean Vanier's affection for him. He is trying to situate himself to her as a protector, since he cannot situate himself to her simply as man to woman. But how can Anne respond to this searching? He is really asking about his own identity but no one can simply tell him who he is, especially since he is hardly aware that that is his question. All that she can do, Franko suggests, is to help him understand that he is, in fact, posing such a question. She can help him become aware of the question so that he himself can give an answer.

Franko goes on to explain that for people who have resolved the question of their basic identity, their relations with others is generally a posing of a question, the question "Do you love me?" or, "How much do you love me?" Even to say that I am thirsty, he continues, is a way of asking, "Do you love me enough to get me a cup of tea?" (at which point Brigitte offers to serve tea and everyone has a good laugh). This kind of question is also being posed by Paul, except that in his case there is an important corollary to the question. He is not only asking, "Do you love me," but also, " *who* do you love in loving me: Am I a boy or an assistant, a man or a woman, normal or abnormal?"

Towards the end of the *synthèse*, which lasts about three hours, people begin to show signs of fatigue but they continue to participate attentively to the very end. The atmosphere throughout the session manifests a real personal concern for Paul and a great desire to help him towards further progress. This personal concern is shown, not just by those who live with him in the home, or those who work directly with him, but also by those in administration and other positions which would seem to allow for only limited personal contact with the men and women. Like Miss Maurice, for example, who as assistant director spends almost all of her time in the office, yet who shows during this session that she has a good personal knowledge of Paul, and a deep concern to help him. It is evident that administrative concerns, and the responsibilities to get the work done has not caused these people to lose sight of the primary task of l'Arche. It is also made evident that everyone, be it the director, or the psychologist, the cook or the short-term volunteer, has an important role to play in fulfilling this task. They all have their particular work that must be fulfilled to keep the organization going: the administration, the workshops, the housekeeping and so forth. But above all, each person has a unique contact with the handicapped, a contact which is unique partly because of his position in the organization but more especially because of the uniqueness of his own person and the way he relates to each man and women. In this regard it can be seen that often those who can have the most profound relation with this or that person is precisely the one whose relationship is not structured by an official role such as nurse, psychologist, or the like. Those who have the least official position in the community must, more than anyone else, relate to the handicapped under no other title than person to person. Thus one very important dynamic of the *synthèse* is the way it keeps before the eyes of the assistants the primary task of the community. At the same time it keeps everyone aware of his responsibility in achieving this task, a responsibility which does not depend simply on one's office but more importantly on one's uniqueness as a person.

Another aspect of this same dynamic is the way the *synthèse* tends to develop mutual respect among the assistants. Each is made more aware of his own unique role in the community and so, at the same time, of the unique role of each of the others. There is a deepening knowledge of the other assistants which also helps develop this mutual respect. As the various assistants speak of their relationship with a particular man or woman, they are manifesting themselves to others in an indirect but very personal way. While some of these people might be extremely reticent to speak about themselves in a group, their responsibility and desire to help someone urges them to speak. So we have, for instance, assistants who have only fairly recently arrived from North America, and who can express themselves in French only poorly and with great difficulty, yet who sometimes very courageously make the effort to say something that may prove helpful. On the other hand, the French assistants, in spite of whatever pain they might feel in hearing their beloved language so badly mutilated, will listen with interest, and rarely manifest their impatience. A respectful listening is perhaps what especially marks these sessions. It seems that Dr. Franko does much to encourage this by his own attitude of great respect for whatever anyone might have to say, whether it be Jean Vanier who is speaking or a young volunteer just shortly arrived at l'Arche.

Part of this respect for the others is generated by a deepening awareness of one's personal limitations and inability to be of much help to a particular person without the aid of the other assistants. I have been able to verify this by my own experience in this regard which I am sure is not unique. When it came time for me to speak of my relationship to Paul, I spoke rather proudly of how good this relationship is. My presence seems to be a source of assurance for him; I do not seem to threaten him. However, during the course of the *synthèse*, I became increasingly aware that simply having a friendly relationship with Paul is not enough. It can simply be a matter of seeking one's own self-gratification. It is very gratifying to have the men and women respond positively to you. If the relationship is healthy it should be evolving, or at least open to evolving. Furthermore, a relationship of animosity might be one that can prove very helpful. It must, in Paul's case, be not only one that assures him that he is loved, but also that helps him come to know who it is you love in loving him. His problem of self-identity could be helped by any true relationship, even if it is not one of love in the strict sense of the word. Also, as I came to know more of Paul's background, his relationships with others, his evolution, his great personal suffering, I acquired an even greater respect and love for him. There was a new awareness of all the complexities that go to make up this or any other person. So at the same time as realizing the importance of my own relationship with him, I also came to realize how limited it was with regard to helping him grow. It was only one of a network of relationships, all of which were important. But not only did I realize my own poverty in trying to respond to the depth and needs of this person, but the poverty of all of us, director, psychiatrist, and assistants together as a team. We are confronted with all the richness and mystery of a person. We have done nothing more than be a slight help in providing an atmosphere that has enabled him to make considerable progress. We can do only very little now in continuing to favour the progress which he alone is capable of assuring.

In concluding this issue we should note that the *synthèse* is, in some ways, one of the aspects of l'Arche least likely to manifest something about the heart of this community. The basic means taken at l'Arche to help the mentally handicapped is simply to accept them as fellow human beings and enter into communion with them on all levels of life, work and worship. The *synthèse*, perhaps more than any other institution at l'Arche, emphasizes the distinction between the handicapped and those who are there to help them. Only this latter group participates in this meeting, and they discuss in a somewhat clinical way the handicapped and their problems. However, this meeting does not tend to reduce the person being considered to a mere case, or a problem to be resolved. The end result is rather to generate a deeper knowledge and respect of the person.

First of all, given the size of the community, no particular individual, except for rare exceptions, is considered in a *synthèse* more than about twice a year, and some even much less frequently if at all. It is primarily for those who are going through a particularly significant period of transition at which time it is important that there be a special vigilance towards them in order to favour whatever evolution may be taking place.

More than anything else, the *synthèse* tends to show the normality of the mentally handicapped. Attitudes or behaviour which to the stranger might appear rather odd are seen, by those who come to know the person, to be quite normal, relative to the person himself and all that has gone into making him what he is. It is often a very humbling experience to see with what courage a person is struggling to make something of his life in spite of his limited capacities, and especially in view of all that he has suffered in terms of broken home situations, mental institutions, and humiliating rejection from almost everyone he has encountered. Furthermore, one becomes more aware of one's own handicaps that limit or obstruct the way he can relate to others, especially to a man or woman he is trying to help.

Ultimately, however, it is not this analytic approach that does most for keeping alive in the minds of the assistants why they are at l'Arche. It is rather the day-to-day contact with the handicapped themselves. It is not in analysing Paul, for example, that I and others have come to know and love him. It has been in sharing life with him, accepting him as he is and being enriched by him. Because this acceptance is already there, when we come together for the *synthèse* we are already united by our common concern for him. Those who have less knowledge and respect for him are helped towards more by those who know and love him more deeply.

Finally, each *synthèse* forces the group to a common question: "How much do we love this person?" The question is there implicitly, and the burden of it is felt most strongly when in fact the person being considered seems to have little that is humanly attractive. Here we begin to discern the limits of a purely human love and the need to pass beyond the techniques of the human sciences. The experience of one's personal poverty and the poverty of the group to respond to the deepest needs of any particular one of the men and women is a kind of call. It is a call that comes from the depths of his or her person, demanding something that we do not have in ourselves, something we in turn must seek from elsewhere.

This chapter is effectively concluded, but the reader might be interested in what has become of our friend Paul. For the next year-and-a-half following the *synthèse* just described there was little evident change in him. However, about six months ago he began to enter into a deeper friendship with Marie, an assistant in his home. Marie is precisely this kind of fragile and unstructured person to whom we have occasionally referred. She has no particular role as head of a household or nurse or teacher. She is just there to share in the life as Marie. A sincere love began to grow between her and Paul. Her own insecurity has made it difficult for her to know how to handle this experience but nevertheless it has been the key to an extraordinary evolution in Paul. Loving and being loved by a woman who bears no other title to qualify the relationship has finally answered for Paul the basic question of his own identity. The rigidity and hardness that he projected because of his fear and insecurity has disappeared, revealing the charm and tenderness that in the past he had only rarely been able to show. He has become a very confident and peaceful man radiating much warmth. The deep faith in God that he always had is again being openly expressed. For a long time he had ceased going to Church or participating in any external forms of worship, not because of a lack of faith but out of a fear of being identified with the other handicapped there. Nine years ago Paul came to l'Arche unable to smile "because no one had ever taught me how." Now in a very beautiful way he is teaching others how to smile.

Teamwork: camping out (*top*);
"*à la vaiselle!*" in the kitchen at l'Arche.

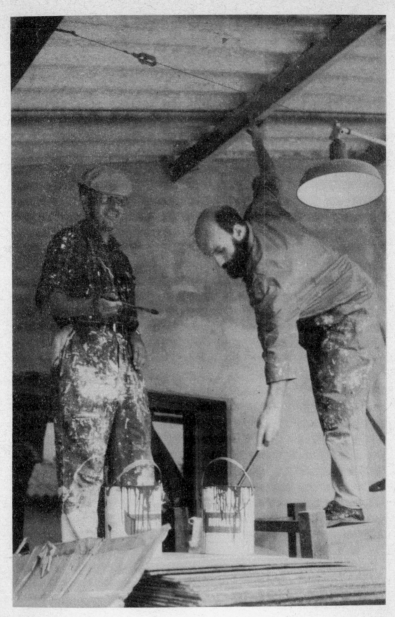

Daniel helps prepare a new home.

CHAPTER SEVEN

Enough Room for Joy

Along with the suffering that is so much a part of the daily life at l'Arche there is an overall spirit of joy that, to some extent at least, is born of the very suffering itself. Although the joy is, in its profoundest forms, a pervading spirit in the community, it is especially expressed and nourished by moments of celebration. As Jean Vanier noted in a talk he gave recently to the community:

> But in addition to the daily life there is also the celebration – this is, as it were, the summit of community life. This is found already after a fashion, in the meals, the songs, and the encounters at the Eucharist. But there are times in the year when it is more intense: Christmas, Easter, birthdays, departures and arrivals, visits, Sundays, vacations, weekends, pilgrimages – celebrations which are not compensations for daily tedium, but which are like the flower which blossoms on the stem of everyday life.

He goes on to describe the effects of celebration on the individuals and the community as a whole:

> The celebration is that which relaxes the person in the depths of his sensibilities, that which opens him to others and to the universe. It softens hardness of heart and spirit. It creates unity between persons. It is the sign of the happiness of the eternal celebration.

It is hardly possible to take each of these many instances of celebration and show that in fact they achieve the sort of things that Vanier suggests, but it will be helpful to try and look at some of them a little more closely.

In general this life of celebration has two centres of focus: the home and the chapel. We shall begin by considering the former. In the same talk just cited, Vanier goes on to say:

> These *fêtes* (celebrations), just as the community spirit, imply a whole world of symbols, a "liturgy" of life. It is up to the whole of the community to live these symbols, and to the home to develop their own style of life – each one a little different from the others – and to create a feeling of belonging to the community. Thus it is good that each home develop its "liturgy" of meals, prayer in common, get-togethers, etc.

In fact, each home at l'Arche has its own unique spirit, but one discovers in each of them an underlying peace and joy. The home is above all a place to be. It gives to both the handicapped and the assistants a sense of belonging. This is especially important for the former, most of whom have suffered greatly from the lack of any experience of belonging somewhere and to someone. For many of them it is their first experience of having a home that they can call their own, and where they do not have to measure-up to brighter brothers and sisters, or to more conforming inmates in some institution. This is seen in the importance they give to inviting guests to come to their home for dinner, guests from one of the other homes or from elsewhere. The newly arrived assistants quickly realize that it is they who must accommodate themselves to the handicapped in the homes. It is very much their home, and the assistants have to learn to adapt to the life-style that the handicapped choose to create there.

Because they find in the homes a security and freedom to be themselves, the handicapped often manifest a joy that springs from their simplicity and purity of heart. The privileged moment for expressing this joy is at the meal, the one time of the day when all are together. So the "liturgy" of the meal is very important. The singing of grace before and a thanksgiving afterwards helps to convey something of the sacredness of this moment of encounter. The meals are seldom rushed, and sometimes the evening meal will be prolonged in a kind of spontaneous celebration as people get caught up in the joy of being together and begin singing and rejoicing in one form or another. One evening, for example, when I was at Valinos for supper we got going with all the instruments they could find in the house, tambourines, triangles, bells, and finally with knives and forks tapping on plates, glasses and serving dishes, until everyone at table was making his contribution to the "music"! Also, every birthday and feast day is an occasion to celebrate, and for everyone in the home to say to the person whose feast it is how much he is loved and appreciated, thus deepening his sense of belonging and others' appreciation of him.

Such moments are also opportunities for individuals to perform, to experience the joy of making others happy. In the home of l'Arche itself, on almost every one of these occasions, Raphael will be invited to play or sing. He usually begins by protesting vigorously, looking at his watch and insisting that it is terribly late and that he has more important things to do elsewhere. His watch, of course, will almost certainly not have the correct time if it is running at all, but this makes no difference since our friend Raphael has no idea how to tell the time. His watch serves an important function which has nothing to do with knowing the time. In any case, sooner or later Raphael will leave the dining room grumpily pointing to his watch. A few minutes later he comes back in wearing a big smile and carrying a large plastic shopping bag. He begins digging into this and pulling out various kinds of flutes and horns. He hands his music score to his neighbour to hold for him. If it is a girl, as it usually is, he will give her a gentle hug or at least a loving pat on the top of the head. Raphael has all the gestures of a temperamental virtuoso, so much so that any guest witnessing this scene for the first time might well expect that he is about to be treated to an exquisite audial experience. He might, however, become a bit suspicious if he takes a good look at the music score and knows enough French to realize that it is simply a hand-bill that has recently been left at the door to announce the bargain rates now being offered at the General Store. There is much chattering and laughing in the dining room so Raphael, standing poised with his favourite instrument, a strange looking green and white plastic flute, waits impatiently for total silence and attention. He may only at this moment realize that he has been holding his instrument upside down or backwards, and the necessary adjustment is made without the slightest sign of embarrassment. Then, with an air of gravity and intense concentration, he begins to play. The sounds that issue forth are indescribable, a weird, shrieking cacophony that reduces everyone to tears of laughter. As often as I have heard Raphael play this instrument my response has always been one of delightful surprise. Throughout it all he maintains his serious composure, with only the glint in his eyes indicating how much he himself is enjoying it all.

What is most impressive on these occasions is the way Raphael, George, Jacques and the others are called forth by the community to give of themselves and their talent, however limited this might be. George's repertoire consists of only one song, and yet everyone in his home is eager to have him sing on these occasions and earnestly coaxes him to do so. He is a heavy, brooding person who does not always respond positively to this coaxing. When he does condescend to perform no one is bored by hearing the same old song. There is great delight in seeing George come out of himself in this way with the evident satisfaction he takes in being able to be the centre of attraction for a few minutes. Pierrot, on the other hand, hardly has to be coaxed to sing. He will, almost invariably, have memorized a new song for every feast day or birthday that comes along. In a way, what takes place during these celebrations is what the community is trying to realize in its whole way of life – call forth the best in each individual and help them to discover and realize more fully their own potential. This works in two ways. The group by its attitude of respect and assurance gives the individual the needed confidence to express himself, and on the other hand the individual, by giving of whatever he is capable, gives encouragement to the rest of the group. When Yve, with his hair lip, that makes his speech practically impossible to decipher, has the courage to get up and sing for us, it challenges all of us to "let our light shine before men," however little that light may be.

There are two particular aspects of these celebrations in the homes that are worth underlining: the way they can go on even in spite of the fact that many who are involved might be suffering considerably, and the way they flow so easily into prayer. A typical example that highlights both these aspects was the evening at the home of l'Arche recently, when several of the women from Valinos were invited for supper and an evening get-together. After supper we gathered in the living room, some thirty of us crowded together on the floor around a few lighted candles. Pierrot, our music expert, had prepared the program, but while he was out of the room rounding up the last of the crowd, the singing began without him, though Pierrot soon takes things in hand. One of the first things on the program is a game presented by Christian. Christian, who is usually rather heavy and serious, manifests another side of his character as he playfully demonstrates the game: a lighted cigarette dangling by a thread from the front of the brim of a straw hat. The trick is to get the cigarette into the mouth (preferably not the lighted end) without using the hands but merely by tilting the head or blowing on the cigarette. First Pierrot tries it, and to the delight of everyone is completely defeated by the dangling cigarette. Albert next tries and manages it with no difficulty. Then Dédé gives it a try, which brings the evening almost to a standstill. Dédé takes such games with deadly seriousness, and once he gets started on something it is not easy to get him off it. He goes on and on, and we all get more and more restless until someone gets up the courage to gently take the hat from him and pass it to the next participant. Those who know Dédé well breathe a sigh of relief to see that he takes this defeat rather easily. He proves this later on in the evening when he condescended to sing a solo – a rare and wonderful event, because he sings in a voice that is barely audible but hauntingly moving. Everyone seems to especially enjoy seeing Jean Vanier and Père Clarke try this game, judging from all the laughter and applause.

So the evening continues with group songs, solos, guitar music and much laughter. Several of the girls who were quite sullen and obviously in a state of anguish during the meal seem to relax and join in the fun, with the exception of Laura, who has been raving or laughing hysterically since the beginning of the evening. She gives such competition to Marie's beautiful solo that the latter with her gentle voice is finally reduced to silence. But Vanier turns the moment into a joke by calling for a round of applause, first for Marie and then for Laura. Everyone laughs, including the two girls. Vanier has developed to a fine art the use of humour to de-fuse explosive situations. As the evening wears on, the atmosphere becomes more peaceful and the songs more religious. The turning point is the singing of Psalm 150, "Bless the Lord All You Works of the Lord," with people spontaneously offering different verses: "All the girls of Valinos, Bless the Lord," "Burning candles, Bless the Lord," "Jean Vanier, Bless the Lord," and so forth. It continues on joyfully until everyone in the room has been named, as well as all the different homes and centres of l'Arche.

All through the evening Giles has been courageously fighting a state of depression. Finally, he gets weakly to his feet, takes a step to cross the room towards the door and vomits up his supper, partly on the floor and partly on Bruce's back. One of the assistants is immediately at Giles' side to help him out of the room. Bruce slips out to change his shirt and two others begin to clean up the floor, while everyone else remains calmly in their places going on with the singing with hardly a hesitation, all with a naturalness of people quite accustomed to such things.

At the singing of *Les Mains Ouvertes Devant Toi, Seigneur* everyone holds out their hands in a sign of offering. On a similar occasion in another home it was Ange who requested that they sing this song. Ange has a history of incredible suffering. When he was young his hands and face were severely burned. Those who were supposed to be looking after him gave no attention to his burns and his fingers were finally all lost. So Ange had nothing but his gnarled stubs to hold out as he sang: "My hands are open before you, Lord, to offer you the world," yet there was an inner radiance transforming his badly scarred face into something angelic. Finally, there is a profound stillness in the room. After a long moment of silence Jean Vanier begins to pray aloud, thanking Jesus for this evening and commending to his loving care so many lonely people in the world who do not experience this kind of joy and friendship. A couple of other people add their prayers, then there is another long, prayerful silence and all join hands to sing the Our Father. Then there are a few joyful moments of leave-taking and saying good night, hugging and handshaking.

Sometimes these evening get-togethers in the homes have a specifically religious orientation. Once a month there is a "spiritual weekend" at which time Père Thomas gives a conference and one of the homes prepares an evening get-together. These weekends may coincide with important liturgical feasts, but in any case, there is often a "vigil" (a prayerful get-together) on the eve of the more important feasts. On the eve of the departure of a group going on pilgrimage to La Salette there was a vigil held at La Source. This home, being the former village hotel, has a living room large enough to easily accommodate the sixty to seventy people who came for this particular evening.

We were all spread in a large circle, two or three rows deep, to leave the center of the room clear. After an opening song, the scene of the apparition at La Salette of the Blessed Virgin to the two children, Maxime and Melany, was acted out. These evenings often include such a presentation. This is done with a certain seriousness but there is usually some humour in it, intentionally or otherwise. When Maxime and Melaney come into the room driving their cows before them there is so much laughter that we can hardly hear Hubert who is narrating the scene. The cows are a half dozen men on all fours, with blankets or sacks thrown over them to make them look a little bit like cows, or at least a little less like men on all fours. When the two children fall asleep, the cows wander off. Five of the six manage to find the kitchen door and disappear from the scene, but the sixth cow has his blanket too far over his eyes to see where he is going. After wandering around the room for a minute or so, with everyone happily trying to point him in the right direction, this cow, in exasperation, stands up on his hind legs and slinks off to the kitchen – looking very much like a young man named Stephen. This all but stops the show. Maxime and Melaney awake and begin looking for their cows, when suddenly at the kitchen door there is the apparition. The Blessed Virgin is there in her blue cloak and with the gentle features of Daniel. There are a few giggles, but there is something very convincing in the very gentleness and shyness of Daniel. All he can do is whisper his one line, after being prompted from behind the kitchen door: "Do not be afraid, come here close to me." Perhaps Daniel's unique gift is to be so gentle and retiring as not to frighten even the most timid person. The scene ends with everyone singing the hymn to the Virgin of La Salette.

Then one of the assistants leads a discussion on the question posed by the Blessed Virgin: "My children, do you say your prayers?" This discussion is an impressively honest searching to discover the place of prayer in our daily lives. Another song, and then a time of prayer centred around the theme of fear and confidence ("Do not be afraid, come here close to me") is led by Père Clarke. The evening ends with a quiet hymn and a long moment of rich silence.

There is an extraordinary naturalness in this kind of prayerful encounter in the homes, where good humour and laughter very readily find their place, and also in the way other festive gatherings almost always terminate in a prayerful spirit. This seems to be indicative of the deep faith life in the community, which in turn seems to spring from the simplicity of heart that characterizes so many of its members. For most of the handicapped at l'Arche, God and Jesus are very deeply felt and unquestionable realities in their lives. They will talk very easily about these matters: at table, in the workshops or during leisure moments. Even those, almost especially those, who have no habit of religious worship are eager to speak about these matters, not by way of questioning their existence but rather to understand what this existence implies for their own lives.

It is at least partly because of this kind of faith that suffering, one's own and that of others, can be openly acknowledged and shared. Of course, the very density of the suffering that is there makes it difficult not to acknowledge at least some of it, and the intensity of the inter-personal relations makes it difficult not to share in one another's suffering. Out of this acknowledgement and sharing of suffering comes a sense of communion that is very supportive and liberating. Together we can look at our suffering for what it is, accept it, even laugh about it. This kind of communion has a peculiar depth and honesty, because suffering tends to touch man at the very deepest level of his being, and it has a kind of unavoidable and undeniable veracity.

Such a communion is then a real communion of persons, and this person-to-person encounter is a joyful experience. It is joyful in the profoundest sense of that term, the kind of joyfulness that can coexist with very great suffering. It is this joyfulness that permeates the life at l'Arche, and that occasionally bursts forth in spontaneous celebration as well as being nurtured and encouraged by organized celebrations. Such celebration does not need the catalysts of alcohol, drugs or sexual indulgence, all of which tend to impede rather than enhance personal communion. It is the simple expression of the joy of personal communion, a communion that calls the individual out of himself, liberating him from the isolation of self-pity and from the fear of death that is implicit in all suffering. At least momentarily one is liberated from suffering and self-centredness in being caught up in something that springs from these but goes beyond them. However fleeting this experience might be, it conveys at least in some vague and preconceptual way the possibility of a final and total liberation in a Communion that is without limit. So this kind of celebration points toward and calls for a ritual expression, that makes explicit all that is implied here, a communion that is an experience of liberation and hope and a promise of fulfillment in an Eternal Celebration. There is, then, an intimate connection between the kinds of celebration that take place in the homes and the liturgical life that goes on in the chapel, central to which is the celebration of the Eucharist.

Worship, as we saw earlier, is a very important focal point in the community's life. In the previous chapter it was noted how people are brought to and united at the Eucharist, in and through a common awareness of their poverty and suffering. Yet the Eucharist is above all a celebration. The important religious feasts are usually antici-pated, prepared for, and celebrated with due solemnity. Well, "sol-emnity" is perhaps not the ideal word to describe what actually tran-spires at these services, either on feast days or on a daily basis. No matter what preparations may be made in advance, there is always a kind of spontaneity and surprise element introduced by the most childlike members of the congregation that turns every Eucharist into a kind of "happening". But for all this, it is still a very prayerful event.

The spirit of acceptance, that is such a vital part of the life-style, is certainly evident here in the chapel. There is singing at almost every Eucharist, because singing seems to be the unique way of praying for some of the people here, and there are a few who simply must sing in order to express their uncontainable joy at certain moments of the service. However, no one feels obliged to sing. There are always enough enthusiasts to carry the singing, so those who prefer to participate more silently are perfectly free to do so. Besides, there are usually a few people at the Eucharist who are simply physically incapable of speaking, let alone singing, while there are sometimes others too burdened for the moment to be able to utter a sound. But these people find a real welcome and support here close to the altar, with friends who understand and accept their silence and, at times, their tears. As was observed by a student who spent the summer there:

> One of the things I really liked at l'Arche was that I could be with the other people and not be forced to sing and dance and clap my hands and so forth ... You felt the community around you whether you were singing with them, praying out loud with them or not – the fact is you were all in the chapel praying, and there is a real community sense in that ... The thing is that there, well, the difference from where I am now is that they didn't question – if you didn't sing, fine. It didn't make anybody uncomfortable. But it does here. So that's one of the things I found good there – you are just who you are. They have a simple way of accepting people just as they are.

In many ways the form of worship at Trosly is very traditional and ordinary. Père Thomas himself has a great love for tradition and is keenly desirous of being faithful to the dictates of the hierarchy and the liturgical commission. Also he reads quite assiduously the public addresses and other pronouncements of the Pope, which he very often quotes in his homilies and conferences.

In fact, it is here especially that an important aspect of the community's ecclesial dimension can be seen. The relationship to the hierarchy is juridical only in the sense that it has a priest chaplain. Père Thomas is very much a part of the life and spirit of the community, and is known, loved and respected by all. He in turn has a great respect and fidelity to the local Bishop and to the Holy Father. Many in the community, partly due to Père Thomas' example but for other reasons as well, also have a personal love for the Bishop and the Pope. The Bishop comes to Trosly at least once or twice a year to say Mass and share in some sort of party afterwards, and also every year or two to confer the sacrament of Confirmation on several members of the community. For many then at l'Arche, and especially the handicapped, he is not just *the* Bishop but *our* Bishop. This same kind of personal reference is also had towards the Pope. L'Arche has now made two pilgrimages to Rome. On the first, in 1965, they had a private audience with the Pope. A photo of this event can be seen on the wall of a living room, dining room, or bedroom in almost every one of the homes. Many still recall with enthusiasm this event, and the words that the Holy Father addressed to them are still quoted with feeling: "You, too, are called to be saints." On the second pilgrimage to Rome, four years later, they did not meet the Pope privately but rather with some ten thousand other pilgrims from the four corners of the world. This was, nonetheless, a very personal encounter with *their* Holy Father, who addressed to them personally several words of encouragement, who warmly embraced Jean Vanier, who in leaving the Basilica came expressly and only to their section and shook as many hands as he could reach. Among other things, he said to them:

> We rejoice to see such a work being realized at l'Arche, under the direction of Mr. Jean Vanier. We congratulate all those who are working together there with dedication, in a spirit that is perfectly familial . . . We would like to have a personal contact with each one of you. May you at least have, in the midst of this great Catholic family, a chosen place. . . .

This trip included driving through the breath-taking Swiss Alps, seeing the marvels of Rome, outings to the beach and other festivities, yet afterwards most of the men and women claimed that the highlight of the trip was seeing the Holy Father. This paragraph has taken us a little off the point, but it seemed fitting in speaking about the life of worship to say a word about the community's relationship to the hierarchy, since this relationship is primarily experienced and expressed in and through the Eucharist.

As we were saying, then, there is something quite traditional and almost common-place about the community worship at Trosly. It is a daily, routine event like the evening meal which it normally precedes. But like the evening meal, it is a celebration open to the spontaneous expression of a whole gamut of human experiences. Even if the Sunday and Feast-day services are prepared for with some special care, here too there is a spontaneous and unreflective participation. No one asks themselves or others during or afterwards if this is or was a good liturgy. Having a "good liturgy" is not really the issue. All that really matters is to be together to worship the Lord.

Let us try now to experience one of those worship services that is as typical as such an event can be typical. André bursts into the chapel by the back door and, like a wild horse, dashes across to the sacristy on the other side. He tears open the sacristy door and disappears inside, slamming the door behind him. All the while he has been mumbling frantically that he must see Père Thomas. None of the dozen or more people in the back pews who must certainly have been disturbed, not to say trampled upon, seemed at all surprised at this passage of a tornado on two legs. Nor could anyone slow up André in time to point out to him that Père Thomas is right there at the altar, since the service has already begun. So a minute later the sacristy door opens very gently and a subdued André reappears with a puzzled look on his long, gaunt face. Seeing that the service is already in progress, he continues standing there scratching his head for a moment, and then plunges back into the sacristy. A few minutes later he reappears with an alb draped over his large, gangling frame.

The term "alb," which is from the Latin word for white, is something of a euphemism for this vestment that André is wearing to assist in the services. Its whiteness has been irretrievably lost to the forces of dirt and disorder that prevail in the chaotic little sacristy, and tend to spill out into the chapel itself. With a couple of great strides André is at the front of the chapel. At the age of twenty he is only slowly bringing his long, awkward body under some control. He plops himself down on the stool beside me, where I am sitting next to the altar listening to Père Thomas. I, too, am in priestly vestments, since I am concelebrating with him. André gives me a warm smile as he extends his hand in greeting. As we shake hands he says to me in simple sincerity: "I'm so happy that you're here." His presence to me is a Real Presence, that makes me suddenly much more aware of why we are all here in the chapel.

André now begins taking inventory of the congregation, which numbers about forty. He nods and smiles at anyone whose eye he happens to catch. Having completed this task he turns back to me and, noticing my bowed head and drooping shoulders, he gently clasps my arm and asks: "How's it going, tired?" When I nod in affirmation, his eyes fill with compassion and he gives me a soothing pat on the head. For all his brusqueness and lack of self-control, he has an extraordinary sensitivity to others.

Now the door next to the altar opens and little Pierrot comes in for the third time since the beginning of the service. He stands there hesitatingly, wondering where to sit, until his friend Michel waves to him from the other side of the chapel. So he starts across the chapel by the narrow space between the altar and the front pew. He does his best to be unobtrusive, but trips over the feet of several people and jostles the wooden altar behind which Père Thomas is standing. The latter goes on preaching without the slightest sign of any disturbance. Pierrot gives me a huge smile as he goes by. As he passes Josiane, who runs the home where he lives, he leans down and plants a kiss on the top of her head, his face radiating love and joy. Then he squeezes in beside his friend Michel, and the two of them exchange several words before giving their attention to Père Thomas. Soon they are following him with rapt attention.

Sitting towards the middle of the chapel is a girl from Valinos whom I baptized a few weeks previously. She catches my eye and begins communicating to me with silently moving lips and gestures, telling me that she is in a state of anguish, that she intends to or has again cut herself on the wrists, and that she does not intend to receive Holy Communion today. From beside me, André blows her a kiss and then indicates that she should keep still.

During the prayers of the faithful, a number of people speak up, asking prayers for deceased relatives, for friends who have left l'Arche, for flood victims in Egypt, for Asha Niketan and the people of India, and so forth. When Jean-Claude prays that Gilbert, who runs the house in which the former lives, be made more kindly everyone smiles broadly, especially Gilbert himself. Patrick D. raises his angelic face from the comic book he has been thumbing all through the Mass, raises his long, boney arm to get Père Thomas' attention, and says abruptly: "For my parents." A gentle smile crosses his face, but it is soon lost from sight as he returns his attention to the comic book.

The singing is not good by anybody's standards but it does testify to a lively conviction. Several of the fellows close to the altar are quite tone deaf. Their loud raspy voices give me courage to lend my own poor voice to the singing but also make it quite a challenge to remain anywhere close to the correct note and key.

At the moment in the service when we are invited to show one another that we are at peace together, the chapel comes alive in an extraordinary way. Some people shake hands not just with their immediate neighbour but with everyone they can reach in all directions. A few even leave their places to go and greet someone for whom at the moment they may have some special feeling. Even those few people who until this time seemed to have been totally lost in prayer, now come alive with a radiant smile for those close to them. André, after receiving the sign of peace from myself at the altar, works his way to the very back corner of the chapel, shaking hands with many on each side of the narrow aisle, until he reaches his dearest friend, one of the assistants, a very fragile girl who has been in tears throughout the whole service. He reaches down to where she is kneeling on the stone floor, takes her hand and gently kisses it, then patting her on the head offers a few words of comfort, before awkwardly barging back towards the front of the chapel.

At Communion time almost everyone files by the altar to receive the Bread of Life. Some join in the singing, while others seem absorbed in prayer. Gerard gives great attention to the music book he is holding upside-down and sings with unintelligible sounds. He gives Père Thomas and myself a big smile, and then adopts an attitude of profound respect as he receives communion. So they file by, a motley and dishevelled bunch, who could easily be taken for a soup line at a refugee camp if it were not for the joyful tone of the singing and the peace that can be seen in many of their faces.

After the communion there is a moment of profound stillness. Then Père Thomas says the closing prayer and gives the blessing, and priests and servers head for the sacristy as the final hymn is sung with great enthusiasm. The sacristy is a scene of confusion as several little children, a few of the fellows and girls and assistants come crowding in while the priests and servers are still trying to remove their liturgical vestments. They come to see or to make an appointment to see the chaplain, or to ask for a little statue or holy card or rosary, or simply to greet us with a friendly handshake as Benoit never fails to do after every service.

The village square outside the chapel suddenly takes on an air of festivity. People greeting one another as though they had not met for ages, or saying goodbye as though they were separating for months and not just until the next day. The women from Valinos climb into cars to drive the two miles back to their village. The fellows and assistants from Pierrefond, three miles away, shouting and singing climb into "Gougousse," the double-decker English bus that still bears the names of the London Streets it used to travel before being whisked away to France and finally donated to l'Arche. "Gougousse" lumbers off like a giant red elephant with its happy occupants waving out the windows and singing a rousing chorus of "Allé-allé-alléluia." With the departure of Gougousse the square takes on its usual evening serenity, and the remaining people, mostly in groups of twos and threes, head towards their homes in the village to have their dinner. Variations on this scene are repeated every day after the service, only with a noticeable increase in the numbers and intensity on feast days and Sundays.

When there happens to be two or more priests at l'Arche there may be another Eucharist, often in the late evening, for the benefit of a few who cannot get to the community service or who may at times prefer a more quiet liturgy. These services are held in the little chapel of La Ferme, which is a centre for prayer and reflection. They are usually carried on in a spirit of intense prayerfulness, with extended periods of silent or shared prayer. Yet here too there is a sense of celebration that springs from a deep-felt awareness of a communion in a common enterprise and a common faith vision, as well as in a mutual sharing of one another's sufferings and joys.

This experience of communion at community worship is grounded in hope and is a source of hope. The awareness of one's own pain or loneliness or whatever limitations one has is systematically avoided if there is no hope of transcending them in some way, or else this awareness leads towards despair. So it is only with some hope of transcendence that such limitations in oneself or in others can be simply adverted to and accepted. It is for this reason, at least in part, that the Eucharist, the celebration of the passage through death to life, is the pre-eminent milieu where the people of l'Arche are brought together in the deepest kind of acceptance of their suffering and limitations and hence the profoundest kind of awareness of one another. We also pointed out earlier that it is precisely in worship that the distinction between the handicapped and the assistants totally disappears. Here each person appears in all his uniqueness as a child of God, redeemed by the death and resurrection of Jesus, and called into a personal relationship with God in and through Jesus. So the communion that is experienced is a communion between persons on a level of equality. The ritual here is not, as it sometimes can be, a way of protecting the minister and congregation from any truly human encounter. There is a real encounter of people that makes communion to be more than just a liturgical expression. Here André can both greet and console the minister, and Jane can express her state of anguish without concern for what others may think, an assistant can let her tears flow and can be consoled by one of the men, and Pierrot can express his love for Josiane and Jean-Claude express his disappointment with Gilbert.

Such an experience of communion is in itself an experience of transcending one's own suffering and limitations. It is an affirmation of a present reality that brings together the personal and collective history of all and relates it to the personal action of God in history, the incarnation of God in Jesus and his suffering, death and resurrection. As St. Paul says: "As often as you eat this bread and drink this cup, you proclaim the death of the Lord until he comes." (1 Cor. 11:23). It is a "doing" and a "proclaiming," a being in the present with the awareness of death, the death of Jesus and one's own death as it is intimated in one's own suffering and the suffering of others. It is also a pointing to the future, to the coming of the Lord. But this coming of the Lord is not purely future, not purely eschatological. The very experience of communion with others in hope is an experience of transcendent love breaking through the barriers of one's own limitations and the barriers that separate men from each other. This is implicitly an experience of the Lord, the God of Love, coming into our world. It was at the Eucharist that Robert broke through the barrier of fear that had kept him unable to speak for two weeks after his arrival at La Merci. His first words were: "I love Jesus."

There is one final aspect of the life of celebration at l'Arche that needs to be considered, the pilgrimage. Each year since the beginning of l'Arche there has been a community pilgrimage. Besides the two trips to Rome, in other years they have travelled in three separate groups, either to Lourdes, Fatima or La Salette, and more recently to England and Poland. The pilgrimage is not just a religious experience, a going together as a community to a place of prayer and worship to do just that, pray and worship together. It is also very much a vacation trip. This is especially important for many of the handicapped, for whom the holiday month of August spent with relatives is anything but a vacation. So each one in the community is free to choose to make one of these trips in the spring of the year.

Perhaps one of the important aspects of the yearly pilgrimage is the experience of freedom and liberation that is expressed by this kind of adventure. For one thing, there is considerable risk involved in it that inspires an honest dependence on Providence. To take a risk is somehow to be liberated and to experience a new sense of freedom. The recent trip to Rome, for example, entailed all kinds of perhaps minor but very real risks. It meant the uprooting of almost the whole community, close to two hundred people, including those from La Merci, Ambleteuse and Valinos. It meant putting more than twenty vehicles on the road for the three-day trip across France and part of Switzerland and Italy, driving around for a week in the frightfully chaotic traffic of Rome, and then the three-day return trip. With the exception of one rented bus, the vehicles were just those available in the communities, including a couple of fifteen-seat mini-buses which were just living out their last days, and two or three Deux Chevaux (a two-cylinder, thirty horse-power car) that are great on downhill stretches but can be reduced almost to walking speed by a steep incline, or even a strong headwind. They formed a motley caravan, spaced along the highways in groups of twos and threes, moving across the Alps towards Rome with all the daring and determination of Hannibal and his forces – but with greater success in conquering Rome with their love and laughter than he with his pride and power. Much would have been simplified could they have afforded to travel by train, plane or chartered buses, yet much would have been lost with regard to the whole spirit of the trip. The departure ceremony began, of course, with an act of community worship, an early morning Eucharist. Then Père Thomas from the steps of the chapel said a prayer and blessed the vehicles and their occupants – a blessing for which the need was felt quite intensely, especially by those in the mini-buses and Deux Chevaux.

Limited finances also imposed the necessity of finding cheap accommodations. Up until the last week before setting out we were still praying and searching for thirty more beds for the week in Rome, and eighty beds for the one night stop-over in Geneva. Finally, a convent was procured by friends in Rome, and a friend in Geneva acquired the use of an army barracks, so we all breathed a sigh of relief and a prayer of thanksgiving. There is a certain kind of freedom when travelling with enough money to be able to afford whatever hotel space may be available but anyone who has travelled with little more than a sleeping bag on their back and a smile on their face, as is the case with a growing number of today's youth, has probably discovered a deeper kind of freedom in this simplicity and dependence on Providence. Also, we had to bring along enough provisions for a picnic lunch each day of the two-week journey, with the exception of bread and fruit that was purchased fresh each day. So we were free to pull off the road by a mountain stream or in a wooded grove or on one of the seven hills of Rome with the city spread out beneath us and share our sandwiches of canned meat and cheese, our canned vegetables and fresh fruit in a spirit of joyful simplicity.

This pilgrimage to Rome, like all the pilgrimages, was thoroughly prepared for by everyone. All those making the trip were divided into groups of twenty-five or thirty. These groups met once a week for about six weeks prior to departure. They met to consider the practical aspects of the trip, but especially to better understand the cultural and spiritual significance of this journey. Together we studied the maps of France, Switzerland, Italy, and Rome. We studied the Rome of the Caesars, the Rome of the martyrs, and the Rome of the successors of St. Peter. We learned a few Italian words and expressions, saw slides of the monuments, sang and prayed, all in an exuberant spirit of expectation.

The trips to Lourdes, Fatima and La Salette are prepared for in a similar way. The reason why these three places have a special attraction for l'Arche is not difficult to discern. Each of these shrines owes its origin to an apparition of the Virgin Mary to poor and simple children. As a result of these apparitions thousands of people go there yearly, among whom are very many sick and needy. For Christians with a childlike faith, like so many at l'Arche, there is a particular devotion to Jesus of Nazareth, especially to His infancy, childhood and death on the Cross. His life of preaching, his words and ideas, his risen life as Lord of history would have greater appeal to the more educated and the more sophisticated. Consequently, the people of l'Arche have a special devotion to the Mother of Jesus, she who gave birth to Him and nourished Him in Bethlehem, who raised Him in Nazareth, and who stood by Him on Calvary. While the overly sophisticated can even be scandalized at the thought of a devotion to Mary, the childlike still find in her an all-important channel for coming in contact with the person of her Son. The people of l'Arche find it meaningful and helpful to place themselves and their communities under the protection of Jesus' Mother. For a Christian to be able to relate in some way to this simple Jewish girl in whom the Word became flesh is a kind of touchstone of his or her simplicity. That the Virgin should appear to poor and simple children has a great appeal to many at l'Arche.

In one of the group meetings in preparation for a trip to Lourdes Dédé was spellbound by the realization that Mary had appeared to a very ordinary person like himself, to such a degree that he simply could not see why he himself should not be similarly favoured. He kept whispering over and over again: "The Blessed Virgin appeared to Bernadette, but she hasn't appeared to me!" I could not help feeling that it was just a question of time before she did, since Dédé, in spite of, or perhaps because of what psychiatry calls a profound schizophrenia, seems to be something of a mystic. He would stand gazing at the stars all night long if someone did not insist that he go to bed. On this trip to Lourdes when they stopped to visit some friends in a cloistered Carmelite convent, seeing the iron grill that separated them from the Sisters whose faces were radiant with an inner peace and joy, Dédé exclaimed: "C'est le prison de l'esperance!" (It is the prison of hope!) Finally, at these shrines there is the encounter with so many sick people, many on stretchers or in wheelchairs. This encounter with suffering seems to touch something very deep within the handicapped, calling from them an extraordinary capacity for compassion. While there, they do all they can to be of service to the sick, and long after these trips they continue to remember and pray for the many unfortunate people they have met. Here is what some of them had to say several weeks after their trip to Lourdes. "I need to pray very much for the sick. We must not forget them." "The sick are the ones who bring much comfort to us, the healthy. They revive us." "The sick people we saw there somehow made me feel sad. It bothers me to see them that way." "I was struck by the kindness and gentleness of the sick." Faced with those less fortunate than themselves they very quickly forget themselves and their own difficulties.

Well, there are many good things that come out of this experience of making a pilgrimage together as a community, which we cannot elaborate here. To list only a few of these things, there are: the communal experience of a dependence on Providence; the coming together in groupings different than those that are ordinarily together in the daily routine of life, and the living in the much closer intimacy that such a trip impels; the broadening of vision that comes with seeing other parts of the country and the continent and meeting other peoples; the deeper realization of their own unique *esprit de corps*, especially through the experience of bringing comfort, joy and hope to many whom they meet. Finally, it is just an overall good and enriching experience which helps to open out the person in the depths of his sensibilities. This, in itself, is a liberating experience that at least in some deep-seated and explicit way, a greater sense of one's own potentiality for life, a greater hope. Furthermore, since it is the whole or a large part of the community that together lives this enriching experience, it gives to the whole community a greater sense of its potentiality to live a fuller and richer life together, a greater hope in the community itself.

These yearly pilgrimages are a kind of ritual expression of celebration of the whole life and spirit of l'Arche, which help to bring to their own awareness just what this spirit is. They are a fragile little flock of people on the move together. Living in the kind of risk that such a fragility implies, they are forced to live in radical dependence on one another and on the Lord of Life. This they do with a childlike faith that makes little or no distinction between the sacred and the secular: birthday parties slide into worship, worship services are festive parties and the pilgrimage itself is both a religious event and a holiday with lots of fun. For, fundamentally, all life is sacred; a truth which becomes more evident as life is reduced to its simpler necessities, and especially as suffering and death are squarely faced and accepted. So life is celebrated at l'Arche in a spirit of abandonment, that springs from an awareness of their poverty as individuals and as a community, and from an awareness of the sacred mystery of life itself.

The unique values of the l'Arche spirit are brought home to its members in a special way in making this kind of a trip together. They discover that their style of life has meaning not only within the usual context of their little village but elsewhere as well – in travelling and in such different contexts as the remote mountains of La Salette and in great cities. Their way of living fully in the present moment takes on a heightened significance when, for example, they are caught in an enormous traffic jam in the heart of Rome. Then their singing and joy becomes a celebration of their liberation from the external pressure of competitive, technological society, and a desire to bring some liberation to those around them who are likewise caught in the stagnant ocean of vehicles. "We are not going to get out of here for some time, so let us just enjoy being here." What other response could one expect from a group with its Dédés, who can be ecstatic with the beauty of a shattered windshield? And with its Moniques, who can accept the death of a beloved brother very painfully but with an extraordinary peace and joy that springs from a certainty that he is now with the Lord? So the stay in Rome was an experience of the way their own lifestyle gave them a kind of freedom that many others did not seem to have. Their lack of money, for example, made it clear that the admission fee to visit the Coliseum simply could not apply to them. So they sang and chanted and regaled the attendants until the latter happily allowed them to enter free of charge. In visiting the ruins of the ancient Roman port of Ostia, here again the admittance fee was waived due to the group's insistence expressed in song and laughter. This was helped by some uniquely Italian diplomacy carried on by our friend, Henry, who has mastered both the language and histrionics of that country. Entering the beautiful amphitheatre of Ostia, with its grassy floor stretched out beneath the deep-blue Italian sky, was not an invitation to study the architecture or take photos like typical tourists but to break into a gay and spontaneous folk dance. Jean Vanier himself became boyishly immersed in the fun, like someone who had not the slightest care in the world.

All this is not to imply any scorn for people who are immersed in a competitive, technological society; nor is it to imply that the people of l'Arche are totally liberated from all this. But to celebrate life in the face of the burdens of existence is to experience at least the beginning of a true liberation, and to declare for oneself and for others a hope that is grounded in the preciousness of life and the undying worth of the human person. It is this kind of celebration that Henri Nouwen qualifies as being truly Christian:

> When we speak about celebration we tend rather easily to bring to mind happy, pleasant, gay festivities in which we can forget for a while the hardships of life and immerse ourselves in an atmosphere of music, dance, drinks, laughter, and a lot of cozy small-talk. But celebration in the Christian sense has very little to to with this. Celebration is only possible through the deep realization that life and death are never found completely separate. Celebration can only really come about where fear and love, joy and sorrow, tears and smiles can exist together. Celebration is the acceptance of life in a constantly increasing awareness of its preciousness. And life is precious not only because it can be seen, touched, and tasted, but also because it will be gone one day. (*Creative Ministry*, p. 91)

CHAPTER EIGHT

How to Build Your Own Ark

Sometime after I had left Trosly to resume a quite different way of life here in Canada, someone asked me if I missed l'Arche. The answer which came very spontaneously surprised even me: "I'm still at l'Arche." This truth has grown on me. Once one has experienced this community there is a sense in which he always remains a part of it. L'Arche is not a place, but rather a way of life.

Although much has been said in these pages about this "new type of community," it is really quite simple and ordinary. This very fact is what prevents me and others who have been there from ever leaving it completely. Basically it is a group of ordinary people living an intense life of personal relationships. Once a person has entered into this way of life, he is held in it by the bonds of friendship even though he may be separated by distance or activity. Furthermore, a life of deep personal relationships can be lived almost anywhere. There is no need to go to Trosly or any other of the l'Arche centres for this. The fundamental meaning of l'Arche is that community is a gift given to me where I am. It begins with the recognition of the uniqueness of myself and each of those around me and the commitment to overcome the barriers that separate us so that we can celebrate life together.

Ordinary it is, yet people leaving l'Arche invariably experience considerable difficulty resuming life in our society. This fact perhaps reveals more about our society than it does about l'Arche. One young woman who had lived there for almost a year says:

> I think the biggest thing for me was that I found so many of what I feel are really true relationships, really deep relationships. It was something differ-

ent for me. I had time to really think about life, what it was. I thought I knew all about it – well, I've been to university and I had all the answers. I found that until I changed somewhat I couldn't really communicate with those people. You have to throw off a lot of your former ideas. It was kind of funny – because you're busy working all the time and yet that's when I had time to think, when I was really busy. You're with these people all the time and you question it you know – Why am I doing this? Why are they doing this? There must be a reason. Well, when I really started to think is when I realized I was so happy – and then you look at your surroundings and it's completely foreign to what most of us Canadians have, and you can't help but wonder – well, there must be something deeper here.

The transition is often spoken of in terms of having been more fully alive at l'Arche than one can easily be elsewhere. One man says: "When I got back to Canada many of the things we talked about and did were just not that important. There I felt more involved with living." Another speaks in similar terms:

I noticed a real change when I got back (to Canada). Things seemed so – artificial, almost. I sort of felt like I was being kind of forced into a – a world of make-believe. Because at Trosly I found I could really just be myself, and be pretty relaxed. But back here you get all these outside pressures on you, and it just kind of felt artificial.

The community of l'Arche has given people a greater fullness of life which sensitizes them to the aspects of our society that tend to diminish life, to dehumanize rather than humanize.

For all of these people there is a struggle to come to terms with this conflict. The tension is resolved for some by their sharing in other forms of community that continue to sustain them. Some have begun or joined l'Arche communities elsewhere, or have simply returned to Trosly. Others do manage to take up their former way of life but usually there is a difference. Like a lawyer and his family who spent a year at Trosly. They then returned to their home and work but, as they told me, with much less concern about success or failure and able to live more simply. A few people, even several years later, are still unsettled and in search of a way of life that can satisfy them. What I have found especially remarkable in meeting so many of these people is that, no matter how difficult the transition may be for them, none conclude that they should not have gone to Trosly. Even people who found the life quite difficult and were rather unhappy there, once they leave l'Arche, look back on it as a very enriching experience. As much as they may have felt out of place at l'Arche, they still have the problem of this transition back to "normal" society. So which of these ways of living is actually more normal?

The kind of tension that is experienced by people leaving l'Arche is by no means limited to them. The dehumanizing aspects of our society are being more acutely experienced by most people. There is an increasing hunger for the joy that comes from the freedom of being more oneself, of being more fully alive. L'Arche is at least one indication that such joy can still be had. It is a message of hope proclaiming that there is an alternative to submitting to those aspects of our society that negate this joy by turning people in on themselves.

This, of course, is not to say that the contrast is black and white, with people finding great wholeness through l'Arche and little or no human fulfillment in our technological society; technology offers immense benefits for the whole of mankind. Certainly the l'Arche communities have no monopoly on joy and freedom, and, most of them are well rooted in a technological society. The issue is more a question of the conditions which favour or militate against a greater fullness of human living, and the criteria by which these conditions can be recognized.

The conditions that favour a more human way of living are threatened in our society by the overpowering drive for a more comfortable way of living. Comfort, of course, is a good thing; but it can become a kind of ultimate value in a consumer society. And consume we must, at an ever-increasing rate. This is the very economic base on which technological society is presently being constructed. The economy must continue to grow at a certain rate, so we must continue to increase production at a certain rate, and consequently must continue to increase consumption at that same rate. This rate of consumption is stimulated by a bombardment through the mass-media, geared to convincing us of all the things we need and simply cannot live without. Products that were unheard of twenty years ago are things we cannot live without today. Furthermore, it is mathematically certain that with this economic base the wealthy nations become ever more wealthy at the expense of the impoverished nations, which at best progress economically at a much slower rate. The whole system makes perfect sense in terms of the economic model on which it is based. However, looking at it from the viewpoint of human values and from a consideration of the entire human race, it is a kind of controlled insanity. It can only lead to human destruction.

In more lucid moments most people sense the insanity of this way

135

of life and the inevitable destruction to which it is leading us. But it is very difficult to face this issue squarely when one is drowning in this world of consumption. Fearing the approach of death we try to hide behind the walls of comforting goods that give us a sense that all is secure.

The security that comes from this world of comfort is really most tenuous, and actually leads to a worse death than the one that is being escaped. The human person himself is consumed in a world of consumer goods. Our lives are outside of ourselves in the wealth of goods that surround us. The call of mass-media advertising is a call away from the centre of one's being, pulling a person out into all these false needs. The interior of man is vacated and left to wither and die.

Furthermore, we can easily become trapped in the ghetto of wealth and terribly fearful of the poor who surround us. Then we cannot afford to hear the cry of the poor man because responding to him would mean giving up the security of our wealth. Life speaks to life. Life calls forth life. If we can no longer hear the cries of the dying, this is regrettable not because it is a failure of justice and love. It is regrettable because it means that *we* are dying. It means that there is no life in us to respond to the life that is crying out for help.

There is, of course, much valid pleasure to be experienced in the world of consumer goods, but there is little deep joy. The pleasure is usually short-lived, and often gives way to the pain of bordeom.

Being caught up in a world of false needs, makes it more and more difficult to discover true and basic human needs. So the deeper meaning of human existence becomes ever more obscure.

The joy at l'Arche springs from two factors that are conditions quite opposite to that of consumption and comfort, namely, simplicity and the acceptance of the reality of suffering. The simplicity of the handicapped means that their lives are in fact reduced to the very basics: the need for acceptance and love, the need to create, the need to find meaning for one's life. These needs are not lost in a cloud of lesser needs. Out of the search to fulfill these basic human needs is revealed most clearly what in fact it means to be human. Dealings between people are not merely the exchange of goods and services, and not just a seeking of whatever pleasure might be in it for me. Dealings with people living on this level of simplicity necessarily become interpersonal, a giving and receiving of love and affection, and affirming and a being affirmed as a person. Such relationships are never sterile but always productive of life. Work is not just a means of acquiring more comfort-goods. It has human fulfillment as its very purpose. It is a way of expressing the fundamental need to achieve and create, and a means by which people enter more deeply into interpersonal relationships. Finally, the life of worship responds to the need for meaning by allowing people to enter into a deeper relationship with one's fellow worshippers, with the whole cosmos and the Source and End of all creation.

In opposition to the emptying effect that comes from being distracted into a world of things there is the call from within. This is a call to stillness where one can come together at the center of his being to be nourished from the inner Source of his existence. This call can perhaps be more easily heard in an atmosphere such as l'Arche, but it is even more needed in the turmoil of our consumer society. One man experienced this very acutely:

> My big experience when I got back from l'Arche was a fantastic hunger – I mean it was physical – I ached inside. The only way I could get any relief was in prayer – only by going to the Eucharist or just going to the chapel and praying did I get relief from this tremendous hunger I felt inside me.

What all this is telling us is that the conditions that favour a more fully human existence are those which allow us to live at the level of our most basic needs, and keep us from getting caught in a network of false needs which disperse and distract from the core of existence. We cannot avoid being a part of this consumer society, and there is so much that is of value in it. But we can be sensitive to the criteria that lead us to a greater or lesser degree of freedom. Being more and more anxious for comfort is a sign that we are moving towards enslavement in the world of things. A bigger car, a thicker carpet, more expensive tastes in clothing, food and drink are all fine, but they will not necessarily render us more fully alive. On the contrary, they may tend to distract us from the deeper meaning of our life. They may also separate us more from our hungry brothers and sisters and so finally from what is most truly human within ourselves. To reject another is always a rejection of a part of oneself. Whatever moves us towards greater simplicity, on the other hand, will be indicative of a move towards greater wholeness. When we draw closer to identifying with the poorest of our society and of the world, we become ever more free from the fear that imprisons many in their riches. The meeting with the handicapped at l'Arche has been for many not just the acceptance of the poverty of the other, but also the acceptance of their own poverty and so the freedom to be more oneself.

If comfort becomes an absolute, then suffering is the greatest evil and must be avoided at all costs. We thus flee from suffering and death, but this flight is also a flight from reality since suffering and death are an integral part of the reality of human existence. Suffering is, of course, an evil to be avoided but not at all costs. It is an inevitable part of human existence, and so must at least be accepted when it cannot be eliminated. The more a society is based on comfort and pleasure, the more it must hide away its sick and aged and dying. The more a society loses touch with the reality of suffering and death, the more unreal and inhuman it becomes. Rarely now do people die in their homes surrounded by relatives. Death takes place in the isolation of a hospital, under so much sedation that it is even concealed from the person who is approaching it. Corpses are made to look like they are still alive. The very word death is replaced by various euphemisms.

The inability to face suffering causes great barriers between individuals. If the man next to me is suffering and I am unable to accept suffering, then I can only meet him at the most superficial level, one that ignores a deep dimension of his existence. There is a profound bond of unity created when two people can look at one another, see the suffering that is there and not turn away from it. The person who is suffering and dying is terribly alone and isolated. He can be comforted only by those who have come to terms with the reality of their own death and so are free to enter into his suffering and death. Others can only talk about banalities and try to cheer up the sick person, which will leave him feeling all the more alone and isolated. But there is a degree of suffering in everyone. So the comfort society tends to isolate us all. We have seen at l'Arche that there is a great deal of suffering. But this suffering is openly acknowledged and accepted. The ability to do this leads to a deep communion between the people there, and leads to a real celebration of life and true joy. If comfort and pleasure are taken as unique criteria of better living, they tend to lead away from what is more truly human. They can even lead to escaping into alcohol, drugs, sex and violence if the pain of life becomes too threatening. On the other hand what leads to a more honest acceptance of the reality of suffering and death will lead to a greater freedom to be oneself and to accept others. Trying to escape the reality of death leads to a death of boredom and escapism. Accepting the reality of death leads to a more fully human existence, to true life, because it allows us to enter more deeply into the lives of others.

Besides the way of life that favours or hinders a more fully human existence, there is also the fundamental attitude by which we live. Underlying the fundamental attitude of life in a technological society is the drive for success. It gives rise to a competitive society in which one has no choice but to fight for a place in it. Even by the time a child has begun school he has learned that he must succeed at all costs. There he is pushed to be the best in the classroom, on the playing field, and even in the area of socializing.

Out of this attitude of competition comes the fact that people are valued for what they can accomplish far more than for what they are. Doing is more important than being. This tends towards a deep sense of alienation in man, because he is not valued for himself but only for what he does. The drive to succeed can be productive of great things, but there is not always a sense of self worth that comes from it. Not only does this attitude alienate man within himself but it also tends to isolate him from others, because success is usually at the expense of someone's failure. Climbing the ladder of success means climbing over others who are less successful. The need for security forces people to play the game of competition but any real security is not to be had in success. One senses that just as his success has been at the expense of others, sooner or later he will be the victim of someone else more successful than himself. Where success is a kind of ultimate goal, even the most successful, in fact, expecially the most successful live in the fear of falling from this lofty position.

A competitive society creates a kind of caste system. People are valued for what they do, so those who are more accomplished are more valued. Those who accomplish the least are the least respected. At the top of this caste system are the professional people, and at the bottom are such people as the elderly, the alcoholics, the mentally handicapped and so forth. The symbols of this caste system are the manner of dressing, a way of speaking, the places one frequents and the like. How many of us respond with the same kind of openness to a person elegantly dressed stepping out of a chauffered limousine, or to a man wearing a roman collar, or to a young person with long hair and jeans, or to someone who is dirty and shabbily dressed? Usually there is a reaction of fear to one type of person or another.

Related to this categorizing of people is the need to conform, the need to do what one in my position is expected to do. If I fail to conform I will lose my position, lose my value. Then there is the whole matter of keeping up with the Joneses, that is especially important in suburbia. This matter also touches the very heart of family life, where children are not simply loved and accepted for themselves but are compared with one another and with the neighbours' children. "Act your age!" "Why can't you be good like your sister?" "What will the neighbours think?" These are all-too common household expressions, that can have very harmful effects.

At l'Arche people very quickly discover the human richness and true value of those who are at the bottom of a competitive society's caste system. This discovery destroys the meaning of such a caste system. No longer is it valid to give more respect to the doctor than to the cook, or to look down on the rejected, be they handicapped or prisoners or prostitutes. At l'Arche one becomes identified with the handicapped, with the rejected, and so is freed from the fear of being rejected.One no longer fears losing one's position once he has freely chosen to identify with those in the lowest position. This brings a kind of liberation to open oneself to the uniqueness of each and every person. Thus can begin that marvelous transformation from the fear of the different to a love of what is different. Other persons and other ways of living are no longer a threat because they are different but for that very reason are a source of enrichment that can release or generate great forces of creativity.

The handicapped have practically no sense of competition. They prefer to share with others rather than compete with them. It is interesting to watch them at l'Arche on the playing field. They can enjoy being together just throwing or kicking a ball around without choosing teams and turning it into a competition. Even when occasionally they actually do choose teams for a game of soccer no one bothers to keep score. The joy is in playing and not in trying to defeat someone. How important it is for a society in which the spirit of competition is destroying people's sense of self-worth and alienating them from each other, to make a place for people who are free of the spirit of competition. The handicapped can help to call us into a life of sharing, where the individual is valued for himself and his uniqueness.

We cannot simply abstract ourselves from this competitive society but we can be sensitive to the criteria for what leads to greater whole-ness within it. Seeking security in position and prestige or in com-formity tends towards sterility. The tendency to categorize people or to show greater and lesser respect for some also is a sign of a turning in on oneself and a closing off to life. The more we move to a greater sense of oneness with others, especially those whom our society tends to reject, the more we will discover wholeness and fullness of life. Living in greater fullness is just as much a gift as life itself. It cannot be achieved by one's own power but we can be more or less open to it and can look for it in the right or wrong places.

L'Arche began with the commitment of Jean Vanier to share his life with Raphael and Philippe: a man of position and much human riches committing his life to men of no position and limited human resources. This was not so much something that Vanier did with great courage. It was a gift he received with great openness. That commit-ment and that encounter between "rich" and "poor" was a gift for Vanier and for Raphael and Philippe and it has generated extraordi-nary life and creativity. Vanier was called out of the security of wealth and prestige into a life of great human insecurity. This has lead him into the discovery of another and deeper kind of security. It is a security of faith in others and in the Other. His own Christian faith leads him to speak of it in terms of an encounter with Jesus:

> Living with Raphael and Philippe and many others who have become my brothers and sisters, I began to understand a little better the message of Jesus and his particular love for the poor in spirit and for the impoverished and weak ones of our society. I have learned much from them and feel deeply indebted to them. They have shown me what it is to live simply, to love tenderly, to speak in truth, to pardon, to receive openly, to be humble in weakness, to be confident in difficulties, and to accept handicaps and hardships with love. And, in a mysterious way, in their love they have revealed Jesus to me. (From the Preface to *Eruption to Hope.*)

Vanier's response to a call coming through two individuals was the beginning of a life of community which has continued to open out towards the community of all men.

Community, like life, is a gift and it begins with the commitment to open one's life to another. That is how one begins to build his own Ark to cross the sea that separates people. The more this commitment is to those who are most rejected the more people that Ark will be able to welcome. The challenge to every community, whether it be a family or a Church, is to respect the uniqueness of its members. Such a respect calls for the risk of losing oneself. A vital community must live in risk – open to the world and to the winds of change – not protecting itself with the false securities of possessions, popularity or power, but relying on the spirit of truth and love as its sole guarantee of survival and growth. It must realize that its weakest members are the most precious, and that its own fragility and weakness is a privilege. Strengths are what tend to separate individuals and groups, while weakness is a call to mutual support, sharing and deeper communion. True community is not a ghetto protecting some people from others, but rather a place of encounter where people can meet in brotherhood. Every such community is a proclamation that universal brotherhood is a real possibility, and so a proclamation that even in our divided world there is enough room for joy.

Dinner at Val Fleuri: the end of the day.